THE WAY OF BITCOIN

Becoming Self-Sovereign

by Alan B

FOREWORD BY GIGI

HYPERBOREAN PRESS

2026 First Edition

Save in Bitcoin.
Focus on your craft.
Live a peaceful life.

Contents

Foreword   v
Preface   vii
Parable of the Empty Vault   x

I   Eight Stages

1. Overview   3
2. Inception   6
3. Speculation   9
4. Fear, Uncertainty, and Doubt   11
5. Taking the Orange Pill   14
6. Altcoin Detour   17
7. Bitcoin Maximalism   20
8. Bitcoin Purgatory   24
9. Bitcoinsattva   29

II   The Way

10. Acquire Bitcoin   35
11. Store Bitcoin   42
12. Spend Bitcoin   49

III   Ripple Effects

13. The Lindy Principle   57
14. Health   60

15	Media	70
16	Craft	75
17	Defense	80
18	Religion	94
19	Governance	98
20	Dynasty	101
21	The Raft	105

Appendix A: A Brief History of Money	108
Appendix B: The Bitcoin Whitepaper	119
Appendix C: Further Reading	135
Glossary	136

Foreword

Alan Watts often asked his students a deceivingly simple question: *"What would you like to do if money were no object?"* The point of the question is, of course, to help you figure out what you want to do with your life. What is your calling? What is it that you would *really* like to do? What is your craft? Or rather: what do you want your craft to be?

"What if money doesn't matter?" The irony of asking this question in today's day and age is that money is removed from matter, and has been for a while. Many Bitcoiners will argue that this is why the world feels so broken, so fake, and why most people feel disconnected from reality, as well as the fruits of their labor. Forever chasing, never arriving. *"All wretch and no vomit,"* to quote Alan Watts once more.

Bitcoin matters, in both senses of the word. It remarries money to the physical, healing the fatal wound that was inflicted in 1971. But more importantly, it matters for you, the individual. If used properly, Bitcoin allows you to be a living example of someone who successfully answered Watts' question.

If you manage to follow The Way as described in this book, it is likely that money will cease to be an object of worry. There's more to it than that, however. While the spiritual path might be described as saving you from the inside out, I believe that The Way of Bitcoin has the power to save you from the outside in. What starts with a desperate attempt to hold on to the fruits of your labor might end with a peaceful, content, and fulfilled life. A spiritual life, even.

Deceivingly simple, but not easy. Such is the nature of The Way. Walking it will humble you, and it will change you as well as your perspective on the world. Change is scary, and the first step is always the hardest. Yet the best way to deal with change is to *"plunge into it, move with it, and join the dance,"* as Alan Watts knew. This book is an invitation to do just that. I'm glad it was written, and I hope that it will serve you well.

– Gigi, 10:37 @ 932,364

Author of 21 Lessons: What I've Learned from Falling Down the Bitcoin Rabbit Hole

Preface

"The great Way flows everywhere, both to the left and to the right."
— Tao Te Ching, Chapter 34 (circa 400 BC)

You entered a world already in motion.

Time was passing. Systems were in place long before you arrived.

Across cultures and centuries, this movement has been observed, described, and lived.

Laozi spoke of a Way that moves effortlessly and nourishes all things. Jesus spoke of a path to eternal life through loving God with all your heart, soul, and mind, and loving your neighbor as yourself. Marcus Aurelius wrote of aligning oneself with nature and reason, remaining inwardly free amid constant change.

Zen later pared language down to direct experience. Clear sight. Simple action. Following The Way rather than fighting it.

The Way of Bitcoin is not a new Way, but the same Way appearing in a new form.

What changes are the forms through which The Way expresses itself. Clinging to old forms does little to steady the ground. It only adds strain.

Bitcoin appears neither as a promise of safety nor as a guarantee of outcomes, but as something surprisingly constant in a changing world. Every ten minutes, without pause or permission, it produces a signal. A rhythm. A shared reference point.

What first appears as a monetary innovation gradually takes shape as a discipline. A way of relating to time, value, and labor. A practice that rewards diligence, patience, and humility.

Beneath this discipline lies a simple fact. There will only ever be twenty-one million Bitcoin. And yet there are infinite fiat currency units waiting to be printed. Once seen clearly, this constraint changes how time, savings, and effort are perceived. Many readers report a distinct moment when this realization lands.

This book tells the story of the inner transformation that unfolds within a Bitcoiner once this threshold is crossed.

It opens with a Parable. A story meant to be felt before it is understood.

From there, the book traces Eight Stages. These stages describe the changes that tend to arise within a Bitcoiner as he proceeds along The Way. Each stage is paired with a sādhana, a simple, practical exercise.

Next comes The Way itself. Timeless principles for how best to acquire, store, and spend Bitcoin.

The book then explores Ripple Effects, the unexpected, non-monetary changes that follow. And it concludes with The Raft. A reminder that even the most useful tools are meant to be set aside once you reach the other shore.

This book is written to be perennial. You will find no recommendations for specific apps, exchanges, or hardware wallets here. Those change. What remains are principles that endure, regardless of trends, instruments, or market cycles.

Readers new to Bitcoin may find it helpful to begin with Appendix A: A Brief History of Money. A short Glossary is also included for ease of reference.

The Way of Bitcoin can be stated simply:

Save in Bitcoin.
Focus on your craft.
Live a peaceful life.

You could read only that sentence and be done.

If you feel curious to go deeper, let us continue together for a little while.

Parable of the Empty Vault

"Time, which sees all things, has found you out."
— Sophocles, Oedipus Rex (429 BC)

Once, in a vast realm that stretched across seas and lands, there was an annual festival. Noble leaders gathered with their children to celebrate the kingdom's long history and its reputation for enduring wealth.

For generations, the people spoke of the hidden vault beneath the capital, said to secure the prosperity of the entire realm.

The children grew up hearing these stories of the vault and dreamed of seeing it for themselves. At last, during one great festival, they approached the royal steward, keeper of records, and asked to be shown the treasure that had made their kingdom so dominant.

The steward hesitated. He told them the vault was unremarkable, its story dull and long past its importance. But the children persisted, and the nobles joined them. Reluctantly, the steward led them through winding corridors to the cavern meant to hold the realm's riches.

The vault was empty.
  No gold.
  No jewels.
  No coins.

The children stood silent. The nobles exchanged uneasy glances. How could a kingdom celebrated for its wealth continue to thrive when its legendary treasure was gone?

After a long pause, the steward spoke. Years earlier, he explained, storms and misfortune had carried away the contents of the vault. The records, however, remained. Over time, those records came to be trusted more than what had once filled the stone chamber. New claims were added. Promises multiplied. Eventually, many claims rested on what had once been a single hoard.

The numbers continued to grow, even as the vault stayed empty.

Only then did the people begin to understand what they had already been sensing.

Prices across the realm had been rising. Goods required more effort to produce yet wore out sooner. Crafts that once stood on their own now depended on distant suppliers and intricate arrangements. The kingdom still appeared prosperous, but maintaining that appearance demanded ever greater coordination and strain.

Some had fared better than others. Those closest to the steward, those who received early access to new records and promises, found themselves growing wealthier. Their proximity insulated them from the consequences felt elsewhere. For the rest, prosperity arrived later, diluted, or not at all.

What had seemed like scattered troubles now formed a single pattern. The empty vault had not caused these changes all at once. It had merely revealed them.

In time, the people began to search for a new foundation.

I

Eight Stages

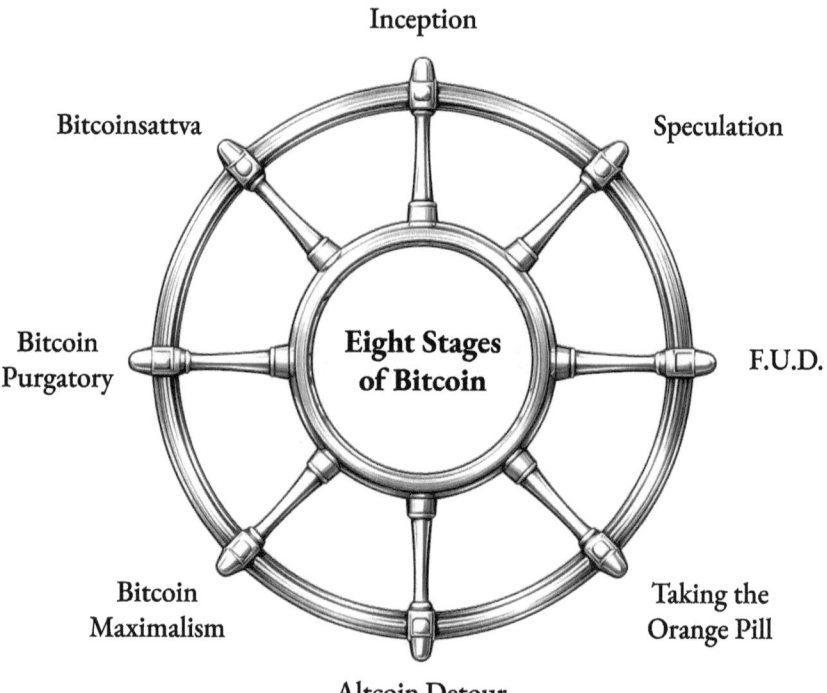

1

Overview

"He that hath ears to hear, let him hear."
— Matthew 11:15, King James Version (1611)

At a certain point, you begin to notice something is off.

Not all at once, and not dramatically. Just enough to create unease. Life seems to be getting more expensive, not in obvious ways, but in persistent ones. The basics take more effort. Long-term plans grow harder to secure. Even when income rises, it does not produce the sense of stability you expected.

You may notice that official explanations do not quite match lived experience. You do what you are told is responsible. You work. You save. You plan. And yet the future appears less solid than it once did.

At first, this registers as practical rather than philosophical. You begin to think in terms of protection.

Saving in cash is no longer sufficient, so you look for better ways to preserve value. You follow familiar wisdom. You diversify. You hold broad investments.

You consider assets that worked for previous generations. This is the natural next step for someone paying attention.

And for a time, it helps. It is better than doing nothing. Better than drifting.

Eventually, though, even careful investing begins to resemble a chase. Gains are offset by rising costs. Progress proves temporary. The ground continues to shift.

So curiosity expands.

You start looking for ways to get ahead of the problem rather than merely manage it. You consider concentration instead of diversification. You wonder whether others see something you do not. You hear about new technologies. New assets. New forms of money. Some seem unserious. Some appear promising. Most remain uncertain.

And somewhere along this path, Bitcoin enters the picture. Or perhaps for the first time, it truly enters.

What follows is a series of stages that many people pass through as their understanding deepens. These stages are not strictly linear. You may revisit them. You may linger in one longer than another. They unfold differently for each person. Yet there is a universality to them.

This same pattern also appears at larger scales, from institutions to nation states. Here, however, we are focused on the individual.

You can think of the Eight Stages of Bitcoin as a map. A way of orienting yourself.

They are:

OVERVIEW

1. Inception
2. Speculation
3. Fear, Uncertainty, and Doubt
4. Taking the Orange Pill
5. Altcoin Detour
6. Bitcoin Maximalism
7. Bitcoin Purgatory
8. Bitcoinsattva

Let us explore each in turn.

2

Inception

"As you start to walk on The Way, The Way appears."
— Rumi, Masnavi (paraphrase, circa 1260 AD)

Inception begins as a pause.

Life continues much as it has. Work proceeds. Plans remain in motion. And yet attention shifts slightly.

Sometimes it arrives suddenly through disruption. A job loss. A market shock. A moment when careful effort fails to produce the expected result.

Sometimes it arrives gradually. As a sense that the rules governing money, time, or security are no longer as dependable as they once were.

And sometimes it arises through resonance. A respected friend or a written voice mentions something in passing, and it lingers. A sentence lands unexpectedly. A new perspective opens a door you did not know was there.

What matters is not the trigger, but that change has taken hold.

It is like a seed being planted. Nothing outward has changed. The surface looks the same. And yet something has entered the soil. Given time, attention, and nourishment, it may take root. Or it may not. For now, it simply rests.

In time, you become willing to listen.

In the Buddhist tradition, the Buddha is known as "the awakened one" because he saw clearly and lived accordingly. This awakening cannot be imposed from without.

Alan Watts once warned:

> "You mustn't frighten them, because they are doing a very far out act. They're walking on a tightrope, miles up, and they've got to do that balancing act. And if you shout they may lose their nerve."
> — Alan Watts, Spiritual Alchemy lecture (mid 1960s)

Most people are doing the best they can within the conditions they were given. They are finding their footing in the world they know. Clarity arrives when it is welcomed rather than forced.

This is where Bitcoin first appears.

It enters awareness lightly. It sits at the edge of attention, associated with technology, markets, or a particular kind of person.

At this stage, Bitcoin remains abstract. It does not yet touch daily life. It carries no urgency.

Most ideas move through us this way. We notice them, place them loosely, and continue on.

Bitcoin is present, but peripheral. Only later, as curiosity begins to stir more deeply, does the next stage unfold.

Inception sādhana

For one full day, avoid using first-person pronouns such as "I," "me," "my," or "myself," whether aloud or in writing.

Notice how you speak of things as they are, rather than as you judge them to be.

3

Speculation

"Hope is a waking dream."
— Aristotle, quoted by Diogenes Laërtius (circa 225 AD)

Speculation begins when Bitcoin returns.

You encountered it once and moved on. Now it appears again. And then again.

You hear it has reached a new price level, one you did not expect. You're surprised it did not fade away the way you assumed it would. Articles continue to appear. Conversations resurface. People you respect, or at least pay attention to, keep mentioning it.

This repetition creates friction, which gives rise to curiosity.

You begin to wonder whether you overlooked something. Or whether others are overlooking something now. You tell yourself you are only observing. Only learning. Only gathering information.

At some point, curiosity crosses a threshold.

You decide to buy a small amount. Just enough to be involved. Just enough to pay attention. You do not expect it to change your life. You do not give it a long time horizon. You are not thinking in decades. You are dipping a toe in the water.

And once you do, the experience becomes personal.

Bitcoin is no longer an idea. It is something you own. Price movements now register. News carries weight. Questions feel relevant.

Speculation marks the moment when attention shifts from the abstract to the lived. You hold Bitcoin now, but you are still thinking in terms of speculative fiat gains.

Speculation sādhana

Read the Bitcoin Whitepaper, included in Appendix B.

As you do, place yourself in the time of its release. Imagine encountering it as part of the early cypherpunk community, before price, headlines, or hindsight.

Then read a selection of early writings about Bitcoin from the BitcoinTalk forum. Phil Champagne's Book of Satoshi, in Appendix C, organizes these well. Pay attention to the questions people asked, the doubts they raised, and the problems they were trying to solve. The housing crisis had just occurred. Trust in financial institutions was strained. The search was not for novelty, but for sturdiness.

Read without trying to decide anything. Let exploration come before judgment.

4

Fear, Uncertainty, and Doubt

"Men are disturbed not by things, but by the views they take of them."
— Epictetus, Enchiridion (circa 125 AD)

Fear, uncertainty, and doubt tend to follow speculative entry.

Many people first buy Bitcoin when it reaches new all-time highs. These moments often coincide with visible monetary debasement: inflation accelerates, scarce assets appreciate, and the prices of everyday goods rise.

In this environment, Bitcoin responds accordingly. As the verifiably scarcest digital asset in existence, operating independently of policy or intervention, it attracts attention. New all-time highs are reached. Bitcoin returns to the headlines. Those who have been watching from a distance finally step in. This is when entry feels safest.

Soon after, resolve is tested.

Nearly every all-time high is followed by a pullback. Price returns to its longer-term trend line. This is not unique to Bitcoin. It is the market cycle, shaped by recurring patterns of greed and fear.

Nothing fundamental has changed.
  The supply remains fixed.
  The network continues producing blocks.
  Ownership remains intact.

And yet, because price is now lower than your entry point, uncertainty begins to stir.

Doubt intensifies. External warnings grow louder. Short-term price movements begin to take on outsized importance. What if it's going to zero?

For those who hold, this stage passes.

Over time, what matters is not the daily valuation of Bitcoin in fiat terms, but the number of sats you hold. That number does not fluctuate. It changes only if you stack, spend, or sell.

For many, however, this is where the journey ends.

You panic sell. Bitcoin fades back into abstraction.

For now.

F.U.D. sādhana

Sit with this question for a moment: What would it take to change the rules of Bitcoin? For instance, what would it take to change the twenty-one million Bitcoin supply hard cap?

FEAR, UNCERTAINTY, AND DOUBT

Now imagine a different game. Chess. You are familiar with its essence. The board. The pieces. The constraints. The way the game unfolds. Its longstanding history.

Let's say that *you* decide to change the rules of chess.

Perhaps you want to make it more exciting. Or more fair. Or more accessible. You add new squares, alter how pieces move, or rebalance the rules to address some perceived shortcoming. You can do this. Nothing prevents you from proposing new rules.

You might convince a few friends to play your version. They may enjoy it for a time. You could invest enormous resources promoting it. Sponsorships. Influencers. Advertising campaigns. Tournaments played by your rules alone.

And yet, almost everyone else in the world would continue playing chess the classic way. At best, your version becomes an alternate game played by a small minority. The original persists. Why?

Because the classic form is already Pareto-efficient. Any attempt to improve one aspect of the game makes another aspect worse. Over centuries of play, the rules have settled into a balance that resists alteration.

Subtle changes do sometimes occur.

En passant in chess and *Replace-by-Fee* in Bitcoin follow the same pattern: narrow refinements that resolve edge cases while preserving the underlying structure.

Reflect on why many eventually arrive at the same realization:

You don't change Bitcoin. Bitcoin changes you.

5

Taking the Orange Pill

"This is your last chance. After this, there is no turning back."
— Morpheus, The Matrix (1999)

The moment you take the orange pill is the moment you become a Bitcoiner.

This is the stage where Bitcoin stops being something you observe and becomes something you commit to. Understanding has taken root and is no longer easily shaken.

By now, you have seen Bitcoin rise, fall, and recover. You have watched it be questioned, dismissed, and declared dead, only to live again. Over time, this repetition becomes familiar. You are no longer put off balance by it. You have your sea legs about you.

At some point, a simple fact lands with full force.
 There will only ever be twenty-one million Bitcoin.
 This is your AHA moment.

Scarcity ceases to be theoretical. It becomes immediate. You see that adoption does not need to be complete for supply to matter. You recognize that if this process continues, those who arrive later will face narrower options.

A particular feeling often follows.
   That you are late.
   And yet, not too late.

Urgency follows. You are drawn to act. You convert as much of your excess capital as reasonably possible. You move from consideration to commitment while the path is open.

Until now, Bitcoin has been treated as an investment. Now, it is recognized as savings.

Accumulation becomes practical rather than speculative. Bitcoin becomes the place where surplus effort is stored. You still hold other assets at the margins, as doubt has not fully evaporated, but Bitcoin is now the primary vessel for preserving your time and labor.

At this point, many are surprised to discover that conversion takes longer than expected. Bank transfers are not immediate. Exchanges impose limits. Precious metal sales require coordination. Real estate takes longer still.

The decision is immediate. The process unfolds over time.

Some people are orange pilled by others. Some orange pill themselves. Regardless of how it begins, many Bitcoiners describe the experience the same way:

You don't choose Bitcoin. Bitcoin chooses you.

Taking the Orange Pill sādhana

For a period of time, measure your life in Bitcoin rather than fiat.

Price all your assets, expenses, and daily purchases in Bitcoin or satoshis. Notice what 0.1 Bitcoin represents. What 10,000 satoshis represent. What a single sat represents.

Become fluent in the language. Sats. Bits. Whole coins.

One Bitcoin is written as 1.00000000 BTC. It is divisible into one hundred million satoshis.

Do not focus on day-to-day price. Attend instead to the quantity you hold in cold storage. That number changes only as you choose to change it.

6

Altcoin Detour

"There are two ways of reaching the house next door. One is to travel all the way round the globe; the other is to walk a few feet."
— Alan Watts, Behold the Spirit (1947)

For many Bitcoiners, the next stage is to step off The Way.

By this point, you see what Bitcoin is and why it matters. You accept its scarcity. You recognize that it is the asset you ultimately want to own.

And then a thought arises. Perhaps there is a faster way.

You now carry knowledge that most people do not. You see what fiat hides. You understand monetary debasement, scarcity, and incentives. It begins to feel like an edge.

If this understanding is real, why not use it to get ahead? If Bitcoin is the destination, maybe there is a shortcut. A smaller wager, made cleverly, that accelerates the journey. If a few hundred or a few thousand dollars can become much more in a short span of time, it begins to feel possible to reach a Bitcoin stacking goal in days rather than years.

This is the logic of the detour.

You notice other digital assets posting dramatic gains. Sudden spikes. Large percentages. Stories circulate. Screenshots go viral. The arithmetic looks compelling. Time seems compressible.

Some of these assets are openly playful. They make no serious claims. They function like lottery tickets. Most people know this. You might win. You probably will not.

More tempting are the assets that present themselves as improvements. They speak the language of progress. Faster. Cheaper. More flexible. They frame themselves as evolutions rather than wagers.

At first, this can feel productive. You track narratives. You watch charts. You tell yourself that discipline and timing will make the difference. That intelligence, not patience, is the key variable.

But a pattern asserts itself.

Attempts to improve one quality of money inevitably weaken another. Systems that appear faster sacrifice security. Systems that appear more flexible introduce points of control. Over time, these compromises matter. So does attention.

Managing these positions demands vigilance. Your time horizon shortens. Gains bring restlessness. Losses bring tension. You begin thinking like a trader rather than a craftsman. Your days revolve around screens. Your mind remains partially occupied, waiting.

You are still chasing Bitcoin, but now it requires constant energy expenditure.

Over longer stretches of time, outcomes converge. Brief outperformance gives way to erosion. The detour lasts longer than expected. What looked like acceleration becomes backsliding.

For most, this stage ends through pain. Loss clarifies what theory could not.

The purpose of altcoins is to separate fools from their Bitcoin.

It becomes difficult to ignore that a simpler path would have turned out better for you. Save in Bitcoin and focus on your craft.

Once this is accepted, you return to The Way.

Altcoin Detour sādhana

When you hear the altcoin siren's call, pause.

Do not act immediately. Instead, write down a clear prediction.
    Name the asset.
    Name the exact time frame.
    Name how and why it will outperform Bitcoin.
    Set the prediction aside.
    Revisit it at the precise date you specified. Observe what happened.

Over time, the pattern is clear. Most alternatives fail to outperform Bitcoin, and the longer the horizon, the rarer the outperformance.

This practice replaces stories with evidence. Ground yourself in reality, not impulse.

Pain is a great teacher.

7

Bitcoin Maximalism

"A man who chases two rabbits catches neither."
— Ancient proverb (origin unknown)

Bitcoin Maximalism arrives as a simplification of life.

By this stage, attention gathers instead of scattering. The sense of juggling competing strategies fades. What remains feels steady. Familiar. Almost ancient.

Imagine a blacksmith in a medieval town.

Each morning, he rises and goes to his forge. He shapes iron into tools, hinges, cooking pans, and blades. His work serves the people around him directly. In return, he is paid in gold. He saves that gold. Over time, he spends it, or passes it on to his children.

He does not need to speculate on the side. He does not need a second profession as a merchant or financier. He does not need to earn his living twice.

His money holds its value. His effort carries forward.

His life follows a clear rhythm.
    Work. Save. Rest. Repeat.

When the money he receives is sound, his focus stays on mastery. His days belong to his craft. His contribution strengthens the community around him.

This is The Way.

Bitcoin Maximalism expresses the same pattern in a modern world.

Bitcoin is digital gold. Like gold, Bitcoin is scarce, durable, and costly to produce.

Unlike gold, its supply is fixed. There will only ever be twenty-one million Bitcoin. Gold's supply continues to increase over time as new deposits are discovered and extracted, historically by roughly two percent per year, with no terminal limit.

Bitcoin can also be verified directly. Gold can only be verified through costly physical tests such as melting, drilling, or x-ray fluorescence.

Most importantly, you cannot send gold over the internet. You can only send gold IOUs. Gold itself remains in vaults, guarded, abstracted, and rehypothecated many times over. It requires trusting intermediaries to manage these IOU claims faithfully, despite a long history of breached trust by systems that began as gold-backed promises.

Bitcoin operates differently. It can be transmitted directly, globally, and finally. When you send Bitcoin, you are not sending a claim or a promise. You are sending the asset itself.

In a digital, multipolar world, these distinctions matter.

Bitcoin allows effort to be carried forward through time without constant intervention. What you earn can be saved without needing to be repositioned, hedged, or optimized.

As this settles, a weight is lifted.

The background pressures of your financial life loosen. The urge to chase the latest trendy opportunity weakens. You no longer feel compelled to outsmart Bitcoin. You no longer worry that Bitcoin will die.

You realize something.

You can't kill an idea whose time has come.

Held in a wallet you control, Bitcoin carries value forward block by block, independent of executives, bankers, and politicians.

Like the blacksmith, you work, save, and rest peacefully.

When this pattern becomes natural and habitual, you are a Bitcoin maximalist.

You are free.

Almost.

Bitcoin Maximalism sādhana

Sit with two questions:
   Is some form of digital gold needed?

If so, is Bitcoin the best expression of it?

Do not rush to answer.

Let everything else fall away.
    Other assets.
    Other narratives.
    Other justifications.

Notice what remains when nothing needs defending.

8

Bitcoin Purgatory

"While we wait for life, life passes."
— Seneca, On the Shortness of Life (circa 49 AD)

The next stage is called Bitcoin Purgatory.

The term was coined by Junseth to describe a state many Bitcoiners pass through. You understand Bitcoin. You see the fiat system clearly. You save in Bitcoin and hold your own keys. And yet, life feels paused.

By this point, conviction is no longer the issue. You recognize the incentives embedded in fiat systems and their fragility. You are no longer confused or undecided.

Still, something remains unfulfilled.

Part of the tension comes from an unexpected place. Your Bitcoin stack is now substantial enough that each new purchase feels small by comparison. The marginal sats you acquire with each paycheck no longer seem to move the needle. The reward feels distant.

Motivation slackens.

Work continues, but without the same intensity. Effort feels disconnected from outcome.

At the same time, a sense develops that you have arrived early. That others will arrive soon. That once they do, everything will change at once. So your awareness drifts forward.

You check the Bitcoin price every hour, perhaps even every fifteen minutes. You begin doing math in your head.
    If Bitcoin reaches this level, then life opens up.
    If it hits that number, then the hard part is over.
    If adoption accelerates just a little more, then everything falls into place.

You are waiting for the god candle to liberate you.

In the meantime, life waits.

Work continues without full presence. Plans feel provisional. Time with family competes with anticipation. The present moment gives way to a future that feels almost reachable.

You are waiting for the Bitcoin standard to arrive.

This is why the word *purgatory* fits so well.

You have stepped out of the old system, yet Bitcoin has not fully settled into your way of being. You are no longer tempted to sell. That struggle is behind you. But peace remains incomplete. You feel suspended between worlds.

Bitcoin content begins to occupy more mental space than intended. News feels consequential. Narratives feel urgent. Price movements still register emotionally. Not because you fear failure, but because each delay stretches the timeline you have already calculated for salvation.

In this way, Bitcoin Purgatory resembles something familiar. The constant monitoring. The background tension. The sense that something important might happen at any moment.

The difference is that now, the waiting is wrapped in certainty.

At some point, the tension invites a deeper question. What, exactly, are you waiting for?

Alan Watts once told the Zen story of Bodhidharma and Eka:

> "Bodhidharma had said repeatedly to Eka, 'I have nothing to teach. Go away.' But Eka was so convinced that Bodhidharma had some secret which he could convey to him, that at last, as a token of sincerity, he cut off one of his arms while standing outside the teacher's hut in the freezing snow and presented it to the teacher, crying, 'My mind is not pacified. Master, pacify my mind.'
>
> Bodhidharma said, 'If you bring me that mind, I will pacify it for you.'
>
> Eka said, 'When I search for my mind, I cannot hold it.'
>
> Bodhidharma said, 'Then your mind is pacified already.'
>
> It is said that at this moment Eka had a sudden insight into the whole mystery of life, the problem of peace of mind, and the essential meaning of Buddhism itself."
>
> — Alan Watts, The Gateless Gate lecture (early 1960s)

Bitcoin Purgatory resolves when you get out of your own way.

Its source is attention placed in a future that has not yet arrived, rather than in the work already before you.

In other words, you escape Bitcoin Purgatory when you focus on your craft. When you recognize your time is better spent stacking Bitcoin than thinking about Bitcoin.

Your craft may be your profession. It may be raising children. Building something small and excellent. Serving others. Creating beauty. Repairing what is broken. Doing the work you already know you are meant to do.

Sometimes focusing on your craft requires changing what you do. Sometimes it means simply doing the work you have been avoiding. In either case, the remedy is the same.

Stop waiting for Bitcoin to deliver your life to you. Live now.

When awareness returns to the present, Bitcoin takes its proper place. It is no longer an object of fixation, but a foundation doing its work while you do yours.

Bitcoin Purgatory sādhana

For a period of time, do not check the Bitcoin price.
    Do not consume Bitcoin content.
    Avoid news entirely.
    If possible, avoid your phone.
    If you must use a computer, use it only for the work in front of you.
    Listen only to music or a non-financial audiobook.

Then ask yourself:
   What responsibility have I placed on hold?
   What work am I avoiding?
   What would I do today if I were no longer waiting?

Take one small step in that direction.

Let Bitcoin remain in the background, doing what it does best, while you return to your calling.

9

Bitcoinsattva

*"Before enlightenment, chop wood, carry water.
After enlightenment, chop wood, carry water."*
— Ancient proverb (origin unknown)

Beyond Bitcoin Purgatory, there is another stage.

At this stage, you are a Bitcoinsattva.

In the Buddhist tradition, a Bodhisattva is someone who has awakened, yet remains fully present in the world. He does not withdraw from life or retreat to a cave. He walks among others, appearing ordinary, participating in daily affairs, sharing the same conditions as everyone else. Still, a distinction remains.

When D. T. Suzuki was asked what enlightenment was like, he replied:

> *"It is just like ordinary everyday experience, but about two inches off the ground."*

— D. T. Suzuki, quoted by Alan Watts (circa 1950)

This is considered a deeper attainment than private enlightenment. The hermit may find peace in isolation, but the Bodhisattva carries that peace into the marketplace, the workshop, the family, and the street. The parallel with Bitcoin is natural.

A Bitcoinsattva understands Bitcoin deeply. The system makes sense. The incentives are clear. The path is being walked. And yet, Bitcoin no longer occupies the center of attention.

Life is simple and grounded.

Calling is lived rather than postponed. Craft receives full attention. Relationships are tended with care. Savings accumulate steadily in Bitcoin. The network hums along in the background, doing what it does best. There are few outward signs.

You are no longer compelled to persuade. You are no longer driven to orange pill. You lead by example. You live your life, and you save in Bitcoin.

If someone asks about Bitcoin, or about money, or about how the fiat system works, you will happily tell them. But there is no pressure in your voice. No need to convince.

Bitcoin has been fully integrated into your life rather than placed above it. It supports your way of living instead of demanding your attention.

And in doing so, without effort or intention, you help others find The Way.

Bitcoinsattva sādhana

Spend a day practicing full presence.
   Stand with a tree and try to connect with it through feeling alone.
   Do not analyze. Do not name. Sense its weight, stillness, and patience.

Notice the birds around you.
   See if you can become so calm, so unthreatening, that they move closer rather than away.

Move through the day without trying to leave an impression.

Let your attention rest fully on what is in front of you.
   Listen more than you speak.
   Observe more than you explain.

Do not attempt to teach. Do not attempt to improve.
   Simply be where you are, doing what is yours to do.

II

The Way

Acquire Bitcoin

By working for it
By exchanging for it
By mining it

There will only ever be 21M.

Store Bitcoin

In a wallet only you control
Hot wallets for daily spending
Cold storage for long-term wealth

Not your keys, not your coins.

Spend Bitcoin

Pay in Bitcoin when possible
Convert to fiat when necessary
Borrow against Bitcoin warily

Spend don't sell.

10

Acquire Bitcoin

"The only way to make sense out of change is to plunge into it, move with it, and join the dance."
— Alan Watts, The Wisdom of Insecurity (1951)

Most people wait for clarity before they act.

But clarity does not arrive by waiting. It emerges through action.

Bitcoin is not understood by watching charts, reading headlines, or debating online. It is understood through participation. The moment you acquire Bitcoin, even a small amount, abstraction gives way to experience. Sound money stops being a theory.

This chapter is about acquiring Bitcoin in a way that is simple, repeatable, and aligned with how the system actually works. You're not too late to Bitcoin. You're right on time.

Bitcoin is a bearer asset. That fact governs everything that follows. To acquire Bitcoin well is to acquire it in a way that preserves this property.

Four Ways People Acquire Bitcoin

There are many paths to Bitcoin. Over time, most people use more than one. What matters is not which path you choose first, but whether it moves you closer to direct ownership rather than deeper into dependency.

1. Earn Bitcoin Directly

The cleanest way to acquire Bitcoin is to earn it.

When you are paid in Bitcoin, no conversion is required. You receive value directly, like cash, without layers of abstraction.

This can take many forms. A salary. Freelance work. Selling goods or services. Tips or payments received online, including through Bitcoin-native platforms like Nostr.

Over time, earning even a small portion of your income in Bitcoin changes your relationship to money. Bitcoin stops feeling like something you trade into and starts feeling like something you receive.

This path rewards diligence and craftsmanship. It aligns naturally with long-term thinking.

2. Buy Bitcoin Peer to Peer

Peer to peer acquisition means buying Bitcoin directly from another person rather than through a large intermediary.

It provides better privacy and fewer custodial risks, but it requires a basic comfort with Bitcoin's mechanics. For many people, it becomes more appealing after some experience.

Think of this path as the direct-handshake version of Bitcoin acquisition. It reflects the system's original intent, even if it is not always the most convenient place to begin.

3. Buy Bitcoin on an Exchange

For most people today, exchanges remain the simplest way to convert local fiat currencies into Bitcoin, especially in large amounts.

An exchange should be treated like a temporary bridge. You use it to cross from one system to another, not as a place to remain.

Exchanges can also be used to convert other forms of value into Bitcoin. Gold, real estate, collectibles, equity, or any other valuable asset can ultimately be traded for Bitcoin, though the process may involve intermediate steps.

Build your ark before the flood. And make sure it floats.

4. Mine Bitcoin

You can also acquire Bitcoin by mining it.

Mining is the process by which new blocks are added to the timechain using proof-of-work. Miners gather recent transactions and repeatedly make guesses, varying a number until they find one that satisfies the network's rules. Each guess requires real-world energy.

Every ten minutes, on average, a new block is produced. If many miners join and blocks begin arriving too quickly, the network automatically makes the guessing more difficult. If miners leave and blocks arrive too slowly, it makes the guessing easier. Every two thousand sixteen blocks, roughly every two weeks, this difficulty adjustment occurs.

The result is enduring. No matter how many miners participate, and no matter how powerful computers become, the network's ten-minute rhythm persists. Many Bitcoiners report a moment of clarity and confidence once they grasp this.

Unless you have access to extremely cheap energy, you are usually better off buying Bitcoin directly rather than attempting to mine it. This is due to the competitive nature of mining. That said, running a small home miner remains a worthwhile way to learn how the system works while contributing to the decentralization of the network.

Regardless of whether you mine, many Bitcoiners eventually choose to run their own node. This is not something you need to do when you are just getting started. The network is already supported by thousands of nodes around the world, and Bitcoin does not require everyone to participate at the same level from day one.

As you progress along The Way, however, running a node becomes a natural next step. By doing so, you maintain your own copy of the timechain, verify the rules yourself, route transactions through your own device for privacy and sovereignty, and strengthen the network by reducing reliance on intermediaries. If you care about Bitcoin, run a node.

Two Rules to Remember

These rules emerge directly from Bitcoin's design and from hard lessons learned over time.

Rule 1: Beware of Altcoin Casinos

Most platforms today are built to trade many tokens at once. Bitcoin becomes just another item in a rotating menu.

This design introduces unnecessary risk.

Altcoin casinos tend to be more complex, harder to secure, and more exposed to legal and financial instability. By combining Bitcoin with unsound, speculative assets, these exchanges increase technical fragility and the likelihood of failure.

Bitcoin-only services are simpler by design. They treat Bitcoin as money rather than gambling. They are more focused and more likely to endure.

This does not mean you must never use a multi-asset platform. It means you should prefer Bitcoin-only services whenever you have the choice.

Rule 2: Only Buy Bitcoin You Can Withdraw

This rule must never be compromised.

If you cannot withdraw Bitcoin to a wallet you control, then from the protocol's perspective, you do not own Bitcoin. You own a claim. An IOU.

This includes products that only allow exposure through custodians, such as ETFs and other synthetic instruments. If you cannot take possession of actual sats, you are not holding any.

Bitcoin's history is full of warnings:
   Mt. Gox.
   BlockFi.
   FTX.

In each case, users believed they owned Bitcoin. In reality, they held promises.

Only acquire Bitcoin from places that make withdrawal easy and reliable. Do not wait for something bad to happen before you withdraw. Take your Bitcoin off the exchange.

Lump Sum or Dollar Cost Averaging?

People often debate whether it is better to buy all at once or gradually over time.

The more useful question is which approach you can follow calmly.

A lump sum purchase reduces exposure to a weakening system quickly. It suits those who already have conviction.

Dollar Cost Averaging builds conviction through repetition. It turns volatility into background rhythm.

Both approaches work. Many people combine them by making an initial large purchase, then continuing with steady accumulation. Consistency matters more than precision.

The Unit Bias Illusion

Many people hesitate because they believe they must buy a whole Bitcoin.

This belief has stopped more people from starting than almost anything else. Bitcoin is divisible. Most people will never own a full coin. That does not matter.

There are billions of people and a fixed supply of twenty-one million Bitcoin. The habit of accumulation matters far more than whether you have a whole unit or not.

Release the idea of completeness. Focus on growing your stack, however modestly.

11

Store Bitcoin

"But keep it secret, and keep it safe!"
— J. R. R. Tolkien, The Fellowship of the Ring (1954)

Now that you have acquired Bitcoin, the next question is how to store it properly.

If you remember nothing else from this chapter, remember this:
Not your keys, not your coins.

You can think of your private keys as the passwords that control your Bitcoin. Your public keys are derived from your private keys, and your Bitcoin addresses are derived from your public keys. When you want someone to send you Bitcoin, you share one of your addresses, typically a new one generated by your wallet. Never share your private keys.

Bitcoin becomes real when you take responsibility for the private keys that control it.

This is the moment Bitcoin stops being a claim held on your behalf and becomes something you actually own. With that in mind, there are a few common ways people store Bitcoin, each suited for a different purpose and stage of the journey.

Hot Wallets

For most people, storage begins with a simple wallet app on their phone or laptop.

This is often called a hot wallet, as it allows you to hold Bitcoin directly while remaining connected to the internet.

By hot wallet, I specifically mean a self-custodial hot wallet, which gives you a seed phrase that lets you recover your keys and access your Bitcoin. Some apps are labeled "wallets" but function more like accounts. If you are not given a seed phrase, you do not control the Bitcoin. You are holding a claim, not the asset itself.

Only use hot wallets that give you a seed phrase.

A hot wallet is an excellent way to learn. You send and receive Bitcoin. You become familiar with addresses and confirmations. You experience, firsthand, how Bitcoin moves without permission.

Even a modest amount held in a hot wallet you control represents real ownership. It is already an improvement over leaving Bitcoin on an exchange where someone else holds the keys. From the protocol's perspective, Bitcoin held by an exchange belongs to them. You are trusting them to give it back. Bitcoin held in a hot wallet you control is yours.

That said, a hot wallet is *not* where you keep your life savings.

It is akin to the cash in your pocket: meant for small day-to-day transactions. A good rule of thumb is if you wouldn't feel comfortable keeping that amount of money in your physical wallet in your back pocket, you shouldn't be holding that much in a hot wallet.

Choose one that is simple, open source, and Bitcoin-only.

Hot wallets are also the most convenient option for daily spending, such as at a farmer's market or local coffee shop, because they are mobile (you have it with you everywhere you bring your phone), and because most of them support the Lightning Network, which makes payments nearly instant, and which has very low fees.

Think of the Lightning Network as opening a tab at a bar. You put down your credit card once at the start of the night, buy multiple rounds of drinks for yourself and your friends, and only have to pay at the end of the night. The Lightning Network operates the same way.

But because hot wallets are connected to the internet, they are exposed to more risk than cold storage wallets. For large amounts, a more robust storage solution is needed.

Cold Wallets

As your understanding grows, and as the amount you hold becomes more meaningful, it's natural to think about the most secure long-term storage solution.

This is where cold storage enters the picture.

Cold storage means your private keys are generated and kept offline during normal use. In practice, this usually means a hardware wallet: a small device built specifically for securing Bitcoin keys.

For most people, a single-signature hardware wallet is the natural destination. It means you hold the keys. There is one set of keys. And those keys are stored safely offline.

A hardware wallet is intentionally simple. It is designed to do one thing well and nothing else. It does not browse the web. It does not download files. It does not run background processes. Because of this simplicity, it presents a far smaller attack surface than a phone or computer wallet that is constantly online.

The only time your cold storage wallet needs to be pulled out of its hiding place is when you choose to spend Bitcoin. You sign a transaction, broadcast it, and then it returns to rest. This is why it is called cold storage: the keys remain offline.

Your Seed Phrase

The most important part of using a hardware wallet is safeguarding your seed phrase.

The seed phrase, usually twelve or twenty-four words, is the root from which your private keys are derived. Devices can break. Hardware can become outdated. Companies can disappear. The seed phrase is what endures. Therefore, it is critical you get this part right.

When those words appear, slow down.

Write them down by hand. Carefully. Do not take a photo. Do not store them in a notes app. Do not save them on a computer. Do not upload them anywhere. Do not say them out loud.

Your phone listens. Your computer records. Paper does not.

This is not fear. It is simply understanding the nature of the tools around you.

Many people later engrave their seed phrase into steel, protecting it from fire, water, and time. This is optional, but it adds durability. Whatever medium you choose, the principle remains the same: the seed phrase belongs in the physical world, not the digital world.

Once this is done, something subtle but important happens. You realize that your wealth is no longer tied to a device, a company, or a location. If your hardware wallet breaks years from now, nothing is lost. You can buy a new one, enter the same twelve or twenty-four words, and your Bitcoin will be there exactly as you left it.

Security, Tradeoffs, and Creative Storage Solutions

Every cold storage setup comes with tradeoffs.

A seed phrase that is easy for you to find may also be easy for someone else to find. Theft exists. Coercion exists. For this reason, many people become creative in how they store it.

Some store their seed phrase in a hidden safe that would require industrial equipment to break into. Some split their seed phrase across multiple locations. Some store partial phrases separately. Some use decoy wallets with small balances. Some hide engravings in places no one would think to look. Some use invisible ink to write their seed phrase. Some create systems only their heirs would understand. There are near-infinite possibilities.

Each approach has its strengths and weaknesses. Increased security can lead to lost coins or complicated inheritance plans. Simplicity can increase exposure. There is no universal answer. You must choose the balance that best fits your life.

Bitcoin allows for this flexibility because cryptography favors defenders.

No one can know how many wallets you control. No one can know whether a seed phrase is real or a decoy. And if circumstances ever demand it, you always retain the option to send Bitcoin to another wallet you control or that of someone you trust.

Some people go further still (usually only in dire circumstances) by memorizing their seed phrase and destroying all physical copies. In this way, they carry their wealth in their mind only, able to cross borders with nothing but memory. Try doing that with gold bars.

This is powerful. It is also dangerous. Forget a single word, and your Bitcoin is inaccessible forever. This approach should only be taken with full awareness of the risk.

More advanced setups also exist, such as multi-signature storage, where multiple sets of keys are required to move Bitcoin, often dispersed across different geographic jurisdictions. This can reduce single points of failure and protect you against coercion, but it also increases complexity. For most individuals, multi-signature is overkill.

A Steady Place to Stand

Bitcoin allows you to be your own bank, and to live as a sovereign individual.

If all of this feels overwhelming, pause.

You are not meant to do everything at once. You are not meant to build the perfect system. You are meant to take ownership, step by step.

Start with a wallet you control. Move to cold storage when ready. Store your seed phrase carefully. Keep your setup simple yet secure. Buy a quality safe if it helps you sleep at night.

For most people, that is enough.

And when you reach this stage, you may notice something unexpected. You feel steadier. You plan further ahead. You move through the world with a little more confidence.

Not because Bitcoin has solved life. But because you are no longer relying on others to hold what you have earned. You are holding it yourself.

12

Spend Bitcoin

*"Wealth is evidently not the good we are seeking;
for it is merely useful and for the sake of something else."*
— Aristotle, Nicomachean Ethics (circa 350 BC)

Bitcoin is money. And money, by its nature, is meant to be spent.

This may sound confusing at first, because Bitcoiners are known to HODL. That is, we hold Bitcoin over long time horizons and never sell. The apparent contradiction disappears once you understand a subtle but essential distinction.

You do not *sell* Bitcoin. You *spend* Bitcoin.

This difference is psychological, but it changes everything.

To sell Bitcoin is to buy dollars. It frames dollars as the thing you want to own, and Bitcoin as a mere vehicle for obtaining more of them. But why would dollars be the goal?

There are infinite dollars waiting to be printed. There will never be more than twenty-one million Bitcoin. Selling Bitcoin for dollars is akin to selling gold coins for seashells.

Dollars are not the destination. They are, at best, a temporary bridge. Your actual goals are concrete and human. A place to call home. A quality education. Time with your family. Travel. Peace of mind. A fulfilling business venture. A life well lived.

Bitcoin is the asset you hold because it allows you to manifest these things in reality. Time in the market is far more powerful than timing the market. So rather than constantly worrying about when the right time is to sell your Bitcoin, wait until needs and wants naturally arise in your life that warrant it.

And when the moment comes when you decide to exchange Bitcoin for something real, realize that you are not selling Bitcoin for dollars. You are spending Bitcoin on your life.

Drill this into your thinking now. *Spend.* Don't *sell.*

Spend in Bitcoin When Possible

The cleanest way to spend Bitcoin is to use it as money, directly, as Satoshi intended.

This is precisely why Bitcoin was introduced as *"a peer-to-peer electronic cash system"* in the Whitepaper. It requires no intermediary. No permission. No central authority.

When you spend Bitcoin directly, you reinforce the circular Bitcoin economy. You allow Bitcoin to function as money. You minimize friction. You accelerate adoption.

If you have the choice between paying in fiat and paying in Bitcoin, choose the latter. Vote with your wallet. Treat Bitcoin not as a museum artifact, but as living money. Make a habit of asking merchants if they accept Bitcoin. Happily pay in Bitcoin if they do.

If you worry about diminishing your stack, simply replace what you spent so your total holdings remain unchanged. This is what's known as the spend-and-replace strategy.

You do not need to spend large sums to participate. In fact, spending small amounts is the most natural way to begin. It builds confidence. It builds familiarity. It reminds you that Bitcoin is not frozen capital. It is usable value.

Over time, these small acts matter more than they appear.

Convert to Fiat When Necessary

The world has not yet fully transitioned to the Bitcoin standard.

Many businesses still only accept fiat currency. When you want to buy something from a merchant who does not accept Bitcoin, you may temporarily need to exchange Bitcoin for dollars or another local currency.

This is not a failure. It is a practical concession to the present.

Some wallets make this process simple. A few taps, and satoshis become spendable as fiat. You buy what you need. Life continues.

What matters is the mental frame. You are not exiting Bitcoin. You are routing through fiat because the recipient requires it.

Be aware that some jurisdictions treat this as a taxable event. Capital gains rules may apply. This makes spending Bitcoin directly preferable, both philosophically and practically.

For those who care deeply about privacy, peer-to-peer exchanges allow you to convert Bitcoin to fiat without relying on centralized intermediaries. These routes can preserve discretion and often offer better terms, though they require more care and patience.

Again, the key is intention. Money is a tool. It is not the end.

Borrow Against Bitcoin Warily

There is a third path that deserves careful consideration.

Instead of exchanging Bitcoin for goods and services, some choose to borrow against it.

This approach may make sense for large, infrequent expenses such as a down payment on a house or to fund your next business venture. By taking out a loan collateralized against Bitcoin, you gain access to liquidity without giving up ownership of your Bitcoin.

In some cases, this can be the most efficient option. It avoids triggering capital gains. It allows you to maintain exposure to Bitcoin's long-term upside. And, if Bitcoin appreciates faster than the interest on the loan, you come out ahead. But this path is not without risk.

Bitcoin-backed loans typically require additional Bitcoin collateral if prices fall sharply. The lender can fail. The platform can freeze. The rules can change. History offers numerous reminders that trusted intermediaries are not always reliable.

For this reason, borrowing against Bitcoin should only involve a modest portion of your stack, if you choose to do it at all. Never place your entire future into someone else's hands.

Used carefully, this tool can bridge worlds. Used carelessly, it recreates the very risks Bitcoin was designed to escape. *Caveat emptor.*

The Big Picture

Bitcoin's total supply will never exceed twenty-one million.

Every satoshi you spend today is one you might never get back.

Many Bitcoin OGs are now living in the shadow of their former stack. They spent or sold at what felt was the top, only to watch Bitcoin multiply again and again beyond anything they imagined. That experience leaves a permanent mark.

This does not mean you should never spend your Bitcoin. It means you should spend it consciously, so as to minimize future regrets.

Ask yourself a simple question each time: Is what I am buying worth more to me than what this Bitcoin may represent in the future?

In some cases the answer will be yes. In most cases the answer will be no.

So spend Bitcoin. But do so deliberately. They are not making any more of it.

III

Ripple Effects

Ripple Effects

13

The Lindy Principle

"However long a person's past collected works, it will on the average continue for an equal additional amount."
— Benoît Mandelbrot, The Fractal Geometry of Nature (1982)

The Lindy Principle tells us that the longer something has persisted, the longer it is likely to continue to persist.

What has endured has already passed through stress, selection, and refinement. What remains has proven itself against time.

Gold is older than humanity itself. It has survived empires, collapses, plagues, revolutions, and renaissances. It has been valued by humans for thousands of years, and will likely be valued for thousands more. Gold is Lindy. Sound money is Lindy.

Bitcoin has not existed anywhere near as long as gold. And yet, among all contenders for digital gold, Bitcoin is the most Lindy.

It was not the first attempt at a cryptocurrency. There were predecessors.

Experiments that gestured in the right direction but failed to hold together. Bitcoin was the first to get the essential incentives right. It binds cryptography, game theory, energy, and time into a system that persists without trusted intermediaries.

Many thousands of new digital currencies have appeared. New names. New narratives. New promises. Countless pop into existence every week. None has come close to Bitcoin.

They cannot catch up in name, status, hash rate, node count, user base, or in the balance of incentives that secures the network.

Bitcoin is the nexus point of digital scarcity. The place where the widest range of people, across cultures and incentives, can agree.

Every new coin inherits a curse that Bitcoin did not face: the curse of knowledge. From the moment an altcoin launches, it is overwhelmed by grifters, speculators, and imitators. Promoters arrive before participants. Marketing precedes organic growth. Shortcuts dominate before stability has a chance to form.

Bitcoin emerged immaculately.

Its early years were uncertain and technically novel. There was no guarantee of success. No institutions to bless it. No central authority to direct it. It arose naturally. That kind of origination only happens once. This is why Bitcoin cannot be re-invented.

The Romans understood the Lindy Principle instinctively. They called it *mos maiorum*—The Way of the ancestors. What has been handed down through generations is respected because it had endured. Novelty is approached with caution. Continuity carries authority.

Once the Lindy Principle is absorbed in this context, it begins to appear everywhere.

14

Health

"What? Know ye not that your body is the temple of the Holy Ghost which is in you, which ye have of God, and ye are not your own? For ye are bought with a price: therefore glorify God in your body, and in your spirit, which are God's."
 — 1 Corinthians 6:19–20, King James Version (1611 AD)

Ancestral Grounding

Imagine your hunter-gatherer ancestor, thousands of years ago.

He wakes with the sun. Light enters his eyes early, setting the rhythm of his day. He moves immediately. Long walks across uneven ground strengthen his legs and feet. His skin meets the earth barefoot. He wades through a cold, refreshing river. He sweats. He shivers. His nervous system is trained daily by the natural world.

He hunts. Tremendous energy is expended stalking, taking, and preparing meat. Food is earned. Calories arrive dense and nourishing. There is a large meal, often in the early afternoon. The body understands abundance because it has known effort.

As evening approaches, he sits by the fire with his people. Stories are told. Bonds are reinforced. Stress resolves through shared presence. When the sun sets, he sleeps.

This is the environment the human body evolved within over millions of years. Movement, sunshine, whole food, rest, and community form the foundation of health.

This is the baseline state our physiology expects.

Medicine enters when necessary. Injury, infection, trauma, and emergencies sometimes overwhelm the body's capacity to recover on its own. In those moments, intervention is a godsend. The advances of the medical world quite often save lives.

But they were never meant to replace the foundation.

Food, Incentives, and the Body

For many Bitcoiners, changes in health begin with food.

Once a person begins saving in sound money, time horizons lengthen. What has endured begins to matter more than what merely feels familiar. The same instinct reorders health priorities, restoring ancient foundations to their proper place.

Steak, in particular, becomes emblematic. The cliché that Bitcoiners love steak exists for a reason. Ruminant meat is the most nutritionally complete food available. Entire cultures have thrived on diets centered around it. No other food offers the same density of bioavailable nutrients.

So why is meat typically vilified in fiat era dietary guidelines?

Because meat is costly to produce. It is sensitive to inflation. Price changes are obvious when measured in beef. Processed foods scale cheaply. They are shelf-stable, subsidized, and industrially efficient. Their inputs are abstracted. Their production aligns cleanly with modern financial incentives.

Once you recognize this, the foods experts consider "healthy" begin to look different.

Seed oils are the perfect example. These oils entered the human diet recently, emerging from industrial processes originally intended for machinery. They were absent from traditional cuisines for nearly all of human history. Today they are ubiquitous and marketed as modern and healthy.

Yet they must be deodorized to be palatable. Otherwise, our senses would warn us that something is wrong.

In response, many return to older fats. Butter. Beef tallow. Olive oil. Foods that sustained humans long before industrial optimization entered the picture.

Once you begin to see in this way, the modern grocery store reveals itself. The central aisles are filled with ultra-processed fiat foods. The fresh, whole foods are pushed to the perimeter. Notice this the next time you walk through.

Life Requires Life

Many people are drawn to vegetarianism or veganism from a sincere place. Compassion. A desire to reduce suffering. A wish to live gently. These motivations deserve respect.

You are free to live this way if you choose. But do so with a clear picture of reality.

All life requires life to sustain itself. Even if all you eat are plants, those plants are alive. They must be killed for you to survive. They do not scream as loudly as animals, but life is still being consumed.

It is also a fact that a human can live on steak alone and remain healthy. The same is not true of any single vegetable. This is because it is easier for the human body to turn the flesh and blood of an animal into its own flesh and blood than it is to convert plant matter into human tissue.

A varied diet can be beneficial. Eggs, dairy, fruit, grains, and vegetables all have their place. But for maximum nourishment, meat is the foundation. This is what every one of your ancient ancestors would have preferred if abundance allowed.

Pharmaceuticals

Modern healthcare operates within a fiat incentive structure.

In this system, internal states are often framed as malfunctions. Sadness becomes a disorder. Anxiety becomes a condition. Restlessness becomes a label. Each diagnosis carries a corresponding prescription. There is a pill for that. An injection for that. An ongoing treatment plan, billed over time.

This is a recent development.

For most of human history, emotional states were understood as information. Some seasons of life are joyful. Others are heavy. Melancholy, despair, and restlessness were once understood as signals arising from circumstance, environment, and direction in life.

Deep depression often indicates that something must change. Work without meaning. Relationships without closeness. A body without movement. A spirit without purpose. These are conditions of life, not merely chemistry.

Fiat healthcare tends to focus on what is internal, measurable, and billable. The environment remains unchanged. Meaning goes unexamined. Intervention proceeds anyway.

Logotherapy approaches suffering differently. It asks what meaning will be drawn from hardship. Life presents difficulty, and the question becomes how you will respond. This shifts a person from a passive patient to an active participant in his own restoration.

The expansion of pharmaceutical intervention is especially visible in childhood. The number of state-recommended childhood medical interventions has steadily increased, yet rates of chronic illness have not declined. They have risen dramatically throughout the modern fiat era. That fact alone should invite reflection.

Once incentive structures become visible in money, they become visible elsewhere. Research funding, regulatory approval, advertising, and liability protection all respond to financial incentives. Pharmaceutical products fit cleanly within this framework. Foundational health does not.

This is not a call to reject medicine. Pharmaceuticals can be useful. Sometimes they are necessary. But every intervention has side effects. Every substance alters the body. Anything that would not have entered the body of ancestral man deserves careful scrutiny.

Your body is a temple. Be deliberate about what you put into it.

Movement and Strength

Ancient man moved constantly.

He walked long distances. He jogged and sprinted when needed. He climbed rocks, trees, and vines. He carried heavy game back to his people. He felled trees. He built fires, shelters, boats, and tools.

His strength was functional. His joints were used through the full range of motion. He stayed limber because his survival required it.

Physiologically, humans are closest to apes. Watch how often apes climb, hang, and support their body weight with their arms alone. Even a small amount of this kind of movement has profound benefits for posture, spinal health, and joint integrity. Many modern back and shoulder problems improve simply by hanging from a bar or doing pull-ups regularly.

Yet the defining physical advantage of humans is endurance hunting. We are built to move across long distances on two legs. Cardio matters for this reason.

Sprinting, jogging, and walking all have value. A short, intense sprint can deliver many of the same benefits as a much longer walk. Time availability determines the choice.

Look at elite athletes to see what specialization produces. Swimmers develop powerful upper bodies. Distance runners develop extreme endurance but little mass. Weightlifters display strength but often sacrifice mobility.

Sprinters come closest to the ideal. And yet even they stretch and vary their movement.

The principle is the same as everywhere else in this book. Follow the Middle Way.

Lift. Sprint. Hang. Stretch.

Build strength that lasts.

Sleep and Rhythm

In a world organized around urgency, sleep is often the first thing sacrificed.

People sit idle all day, overstimulated but under-exerted, then stare into glowing screens late into the night and wonder why rest does not come.

Follow The Way of the ancestors to sleep more soundly.

Move enough so that you are physically, not just mentally, tired. Let the sun set your rhythm. Expose your eyes to sunlight early in the morning and again before sundown. This anchors your circadian rhythm and stabilizes everything downstream, from hormones to mood to metabolism.

When evening arrives, turn off the screens. TVs. Phones. Laptops.

Read a physical book instead. Make it a nightly ritual.

Sleep is not optional. It is the foundation beneath every other function of life.

Nature and Grounding

Health does not exist indoors alone.

The human nervous system evolved in direct contact with the natural world. Sunlight. Wind. Water. Grass. Dirt. Silence. Birdsong. Stargazing.

These inputs regulate stress in ways no supplement can replicate.

There is also a more specific dimension here. Ancient man was a hunter.

That means he would scan vast distances. Watch the horizon. Track movements far off. Stare into open space while walking for long periods of time. The eyes, neck, and nervous system are adapted for this kind of wide-field awareness.

Modern life collapses this range. Screens dominate attention. Phones. Laptops. Tablets. The eyes lock onto objects inches away for hours at a time. Some of this is unavoidable in a digital world, especially if you earn your living at a desk. But imbalance has consequences.

Extended near-field focus narrows perception. Tension accumulates. The nervous system stays alert without release. Time outdoors restores what is missing.

Go for walks regularly. This is natural if you have a dog. Let your gaze drift to clouds, birds, distant trees, mountain ridgelines. At night, look at the stars. Let your eyes relax.

"Touch grass" is crude language for a real truth.

Your body recognizes the world it was built for.

Family and Community

Health is shaped by your social environment as much as your physical one.

Your ancestors did not live alone.

They ate together. Worked together. Raised children together. Grieved together. Celebrated together. Life unfolded in proximity to others.

Isolation is a modern pathology.

There is a reason solitary confinement is considered one of the most severe punishments in prison. Extended isolation damages the mind and the body. Humans are not designed for prolonged isolation.

There is a difference between chosen solitude and imposed loneliness.

A monk in a cave, oriented toward contemplation, inhabits a very different psychological state than someone alone because they feel unseen, misunderstood, or disconnected. The first can heal. The second corrodes.

Digital relationships do help. They are often valuable. But they are not a substitute for physical presence. For shared meals. For laughter in the same room. For the feeling of being known by people who can see your face and hear your voice.

There is also a subtle trap here. Finding Bitcoin can bring clarity. It can also bring arrogance if you are not careful. Avoid the temptation to see yourself as awake while everyone else is a normie or an NPC. That mindset isolates you unnecessarily and weakens you in a real sense. Every person who hasn't yet found Bitcoin is just like you used to be. Remember that.

Spend time with your family, friends, and neighbors. The people physically around you.

We are all moving through space and time together. Live accordingly.

Don't Trust. Verify.

Bitcoiners repeat a simple phrase: Don't trust. Verify. Health demands the same discipline.

You and your body are one. Do not defer to another's authority, even if he is wearing a white coat, unless you yourself have chosen to.

When you walk The Way, responsibility moves inward. Judgment becomes personal rather than outsourced. Risk assessment replaces obedience.

Ground yourself first in what sustained humans for millennia, and approach modern interventions consciously rather than reflexively.

If you have your health, you have everything. When health fails, nothing else matters.

15

Media

"Such as are your habitual thoughts, such also will be the character of your mind;
  for the soul is dyed by the thoughts."
  — Marcus Aurelius, Meditations (circa 170 AD)

Just as you are what you eat, you are also what you think.
  Media consumption shapes thought. Thought shapes action.

Bitcoiners tend to pass through a recognizable progression as they follow The Way.

Media Habits

Most begin immersed in modern popular media. News feeds. Social media. Streaming content. The default informational diet of the fiat world.

Then comes Bitcoin media.

Podcasts. Videos. Books. Audiobooks. Lectures. Hours per day absorbing what other Bitcoiners have already discovered, organized, and articulated. This phase is necessary. It is educational. It is energizing. It sharpens perception.

For a time, it is exactly what is needed.

Eventually, repetition sets in. The arguments become familiar. The patterns are understood. Bitcoin content begins to loop.

At this stage, many move toward Bitcoin-adjacent news. Always watching for the catalyst. The announcement. The crisis that will force the Bitcoin standard into being. This is particularly common during the Bitcoin Purgatory stage.

This is understandable. It is also taxing.

Modern news is engineered to capture attention through fear, outrage, and urgency. Doom scrolling is an accurate description. Prolonged exposure degrades moods, narrows perception, drains energy, and often makes reality appear worse than it actually is.

Those who move beyond this phase change their media diet yet again.

They still check major news, Bitcoin podcasts, and modern entertainment from time to time. But their center of gravity shifts to Lindy content. Evergreen content. Ancient content.

Old books. Primary sources. The great works.

They become careful about what enters their mind. They prefer material that has survived centuries of scrutiny. The older the work, the more reality has already filtered it.

Mapping Reality

In doing so, they begin building a mental map that spans time and place. Not just what is happening now, but what has always happened. Patterns emerge. Cycles become visible. Perspective deepens.

When you primarily consume content from the gold-standard era, meaning anything written before the creation of the Federal Reserve in 1913, you begin to see what the world can look like under a sound money paradigm. This makes old books deeply relevant to the digital sound-money world now emerging. They are also less depressing and free from hidden fiat incentives.

Personally, the only thing I stack consistently besides Bitcoin is books. Physical books. Mostly old or ancient. Mostly hardcover.

There is a reason the Epicureans say that if a man has a library and a garden, he has everything. A well-chosen library allows you to step inside the minds of some of the world's great thinkers, to absorb what they spent a lifetime learning vicariously. It is also a durable reference point for all that you have gleaned, which you can return to at any point. And you never have to worry about its contents being covertly altered. You have the real thing.

Attention Span

Another benefit of Lindy media is attention.

When you move from sixty-second clips to six-hundred-page books, your capacity for sustained thought expands. Distraction loosens its grip. Thinking becomes clearer and more conscientious.

It is the literary equivalent of moving from a diet of candy bars to ribeyes. The transition can be difficult at first. But over time, health improves. Energy stabilizes. Taste changes.

Bitcoin teaches patience with money. Ancient media teaches patience with thought.

People, Brands, Platforms

A related shift often follows.

Bitcoiners become more deliberate about *who* they listen to, and *how* information reaches them.

Under a fiat mindset, it is common to trust authority by default. If a claim comes from a respected outlet or established brand, it is often assumed to be true.

Bitcoin rewires this habit. Bitcoin trains the mind to verify rather than trust.

This does not mean all brands are dismissed. Some remain useful. But only when the people behind them are known, coherent, and accountable. A brand earns credibility when its stewards are visible and consistent.

Individuals are often easier to evaluate than institutions.

A single person represents one integrated perspective. Over time, you learn their incentives, temperament, and limits. You know where they tend to be right, where they tend to err, and how seriously to weigh what they say.

Brands are murkier. Many voices speak through them. Incentives shift quietly. Editorial direction changes without notice.

Mental OPSEC

The modern digital environment introduces yet another complication.

Bots. AI-generated personas. Engagement farmers. Coordinated manipulators.

Strong operations security around media consumption becomes vital. Because of this, many Bitcoiners adjust their relationship with social media.

Some move toward decentralized, Bitcoin-native platforms such as Nostr, where identity is cryptographic, incentives are explicit, and small Bitcoin payments accompany quality posts. This creates a more robust signal and reduces the surface area for manipulation. Others choose to remain on the major centralized social media networks, but are surgically precise about who they choose to follow and what keywords they allow to appear in their feed.

Connection with other humans remains valuable. Total isolation is rarely healthy.

The change is intentionality. Engage deliberately. Verify sources. Prefer clarity over volume. Treat attention as something scarce and worth protecting.

By doing so, you reduce noise, preserve agency, and remain oriented toward what is true and enduring.

16

Craft

"Practice and realization are one and the same."
— Eihei Dōgen Zenji, Bendōwa (1231 AD)

Escape the Cantillon Effect

The fiat era rewards proximity to the money printer.

This dynamic is known as the Cantillon Effect. Those closest to newly created money benefit first. Those furthest away absorb the costs later, through rising prices and diluted purchasing power.

Bitcoin operates on a different principle: Proof-of-work.

There is no free lunch in Bitcoin. No favored position. No privileged access. Bitcoin can only be acquired through effort.

That effort can take many forms. You may exchange your labor for it, deploy energy and expertise to mine it, or trade other forms of stored value for it such as gold or real estate.

What you cannot do is print it.

This simple constraint reshapes behavior.

Find Your Calling

Bitcoin rewards honest, diligent effort and exposes shortcuts. Over time, many people feel this pressure turn inward and begin asking a new question.

How am I best suited to exchange work for Bitcoin?

At this stage, many Bitcoiners become attracted to the idea of getting a "Bitcoin job." They want to work for a Bitcoin company, build Bitcoin products, or spend their days evangelizing Bitcoin itself. If that is your calling, follow it.

But realize this: Every job is a Bitcoin job if you save in Bitcoin and focus on your craft.
   A carpenter who saves in Bitcoin has a Bitcoin job.
   A teacher who saves in Bitcoin has a Bitcoin job.
   An engineer, artist, or farmer who saves in Bitcoin has a Bitcoin job.

The key question is not *How do I get a Bitcoin job?* It is *What am I called to do?*

This is where craft enters.

Craft is the place where ability, enjoyment, and usefulness overlap. It is what you do well. What you find fulfilling. What the world actually needs. When these align, work becomes less about extraction and more about contribution.

Finding your craft is not always immediate. It often emerges through curiosity. Follow it. Let it pull you into areas that invite attention rather than drain it.

Go deep where you are strongest. Develop real competence. At the same time, remain broadly literate. Learn enough about adjacent fields to avoid blind spots and exploitation. This balance is called a T-shaped skill set: Depth in one domain, awareness across many.

Some take this further, stacking multiple talents into a rare combination.

It is easier to become world-class at a unique intersection than at a single crowded peak. For instance, it is immensely difficult to become the world's top software developer. But if you love code and love studying Medieval history, you have a reasonable chance of becoming the world's top software developer focused on building Middle Ages–themed websites.

As you follow The Way, curiosity will widen rather than narrow. Let it. But anchor it to a mission that matters to you. Meaning sustains effort over time and prevents burnout.

As Nietzsche observed: A man who has a *why* can bear almost any *how*.

What if I Never "Make It?"

At this point, doubts may arise.
What if the work you feel called to do never leads to the success you hoped for?
Wouldn't it be safer to stick with something less aligned, but more certain?

Carl Jung reminds us of a reassuring truth:

> *"No matter how isolated you are and how lonely you feel, if you do your work truly and conscientiously, unknown friends will come and seek*

you."
— C. G. Jung, Letters (circa 1933)

Bitcoin gives such work the time it requires to take root.

Save First. Spend Second.

One common objection to Bitcoin is the claim of having nothing to save. No excess. No dry powder. Expenses consume everything.

In most cases, this is not strictly true.

What often helps is a simple inversion. Rather than spending first, paying all your bills, and only afterward seeing what remains to save in Bitcoin, reverse the order.

Save first. Spend second.

This creates a powerful shift. You are now working for yourself in a real sense. And so long as you do not become excessive in the amount you save, this discipline does not harm you. It strengthens you.

Many find it helpful to set up an automatic daily, weekly, or monthly Bitcoin purchase. The steady increase in sats over time has an empowering, confidence-building effect.

Bitcoin does not require dramatic action. It responds to consistency. Ten thousand sats, fifty thousand sats, one hundred thousand sats per week, accumulated honestly, add up.

This is no different from health. Someone who wishes to lose weight but refuses to change day-to-day diet or exercise habits will remain frustrated. The fundamentals matter. Make them repeatable. Make them habitual.

Focus on your craft. Save something regularly, before discretionary spending. This simple practice changes how you relate to time, effort, and reward.

And remember:

God will steer the ship. But you must row.

17

Defense

"Therefore, he who desires peace should prepare for war."
— Publius Flavius Vegetius Renatus, De Re Militari (circa 390 AD)

Being your own bank implies being your own bank guard.

Even if you hire guards to watch you day and night, you remain the one overseeing those guards. You remain responsible for operational security and for how it improves over time.

Bitcoin places responsibility where it belongs. With the holder.

When value is held personally, defense becomes real. You begin to think clearly about how value is lost, how it is protected, and where tradeoffs exist.

There is no perfect setup. Every security decision strengthens some defenses while weakening others. The goal is to find the best balance with all attack vectors considered.

Castle Mindset

The right mental model for Bitcoin defense is a castle.

A strong castle does not rely on a single wall. It has layers. Outer walls. Limited entrances. Guard towers. Inner courtyards. An inner sanctum where what matters most is kept.

Each layer increases time, effort, and visibility for an attacker. Each layer creates friction. Each layer creates options for the defender.

Bitcoin defense follows the same logic.

Your keys should sit behind multiple barriers. Physical and digital. Obvious and subtle. A thief should have to cross several thresholds before reaching anything meaningful.

This applies equally to digital threats and physical ones. It applies to theft, loss, coercion, and error.

Professionals securing high-value environments follow a simple principle. Secure the immediate area first. Then expand outward. What is closest matters most. Then the perimeter. Then the environment beyond.

Layered defense buys time. Time reveals intent. Time creates choices.

With this frame in place, the ways Bitcoin is actually lost become clear.

The Primary Ways Bitcoin is Lost

Listed from most common to least.

1. Loss of Private Keys

This is the single largest source of permanent Bitcoin loss.

Keys are forgotten. Passphrases are forgotten. Seed phrases are damaged, misplaced, or destroyed. Storage devices fail without backups existing to restore them.

Defense:

Understand your key setup fully. Store seed phrases deliberately. Create backups if necessary, but be mindful of where those backups live. Protect them from fire, water, and time by engraving them in steel and/or placing them in a fireproof and waterproof safe.

Do not rely on memory alone. The passphrase you believe you will always remember may one day be forgotten. Store it securely alongside your seed phrase.

2. Death without Inheritance Planning

Bitcoin held without succession planning often vanishes with its owner.

Defense:

Design inheritance intentionally. Ensure your heirs can recover funds. Identify who in your life you trust to handle this both technically and ethically.

Discuss this in person. Go for a walk. Leave your phones behind. Speak plainly. Bitcoin inheritance is not an abstraction. It is a responsibility.

3. Scams and Social Engineering

This is the largest theft vector by volume.

Romance scams. Impersonation of celebrities, law enforcement, tax authorities, or hardware manufacturers. Fake investment opportunities. Manufactured urgency.

Defense:

A simple rule works well. Never discuss your Bitcoin setup with anyone, for any reason, unless required for inheritance planning. Think of the famous line from *Fight Club* (1999), modified for Bitcoiners: The first rule is, you do not talk about your Bitcoin. The second rule is, you DO NOT talk about your Bitcoin.

It doesn't matter if His Majesty the King is on the phone. Or the President. Or the CEO of the hardware wallet company you use. Or tax authorities saying they'll send you to jail unless you comply. Hang up the phone. Block that person's number or email. Move on.

Initiate all Bitcoin actions yourself. Don't do anything you weren't already planning to do.

4. Wallet Compromises

Malware. Fake wallets. Key extraction. Infected devices.

Defense:

Use dedicated hardware for key management. Use open-source or source-verifiable, Bitcoin-only hardware wallets from reputable manufacturers.

Do not store details about your Bitcoin setup on your phone, laptop, or cloud services. In the era of AI, anything digitally accessible is vulnerable.

Keep your seed phrase in the physical world only. Enter it only into your hardware wallet. Never into a website or app. Always verify transaction details on the hardware wallet screen itself before confirming.

5. Sending Funds to the Wrong Address

Typos. Clipboard manipulation. Address poisoning.

Defense:

Verify addresses visually on your hardware device. Use test transactions when appropriate, especially for large transfers. Move deliberately. Bitcoin rewards precision and patience.

6. Platform and Exchange Failures

Hacks. Insolvency. Regulatory seizure.

Defense:

He who holds the keys holds the coins. If an institution holds your Bitcoin keys, you do not own that Bitcoin. You own a claim.

Exchange failures have happened repeatedly and will happen again. The defense is simple. Self-custody.

If you must use a custodian, choose one that is Bitcoin-only and does not rehypothecate. Fewer crypto assets under management mean less complexity. Even then, understand you hold an IOU, with all the risks that implies.

7. Extortion

Your keys are not compromised. Something else you value is. And the perpetrators are demanding you send them Bitcoin. This attack vector can take many forms.

Critical files are encrypted. Work systems are disabled. Private information is obtained and threatened with release. Bitcoin is demanded because it settles globally and irreversibly.

Defense:

Protect what gives others leverage over you.

Maintain offline backups of all essential files. Store them on external drives that are never connected to the internet except when updating. Test recovery periodically.

Separate critical systems from general-purpose devices. Reduce digital exposure.

Live in a way that limits coercive leverage. A moral life narrows extortion pathways. When revelation holds no power, coercion loses force. Bitcoin secures value. Character secures reputation.

8. State Confiscation

Asset forfeiture. Capital controls. Legal seizure.

Defense:

Understand your jurisdiction. Even in the United States, precedent for confiscation exists.

In 1933, President Franklin D. Roosevelt signed Executive Order 6102, which prohibited the private ownership of monetary gold. Citizens were required to deliver gold coins, bullion, and certificates to the Federal Reserve in exchange for dollars, under penalty of fine or imprisonment.

What is often misunderstood is how this played out in practice.

Gold held in banks was confiscated immediately. Banks were compelled to comply, and custodial gold was surrendered as a matter of record. There was no choice involved. If your gold was held by an institution, it was taken.

Gold held privately was different.

Individuals who held gold personally were faced with a decision. Compliance was required by law, but enforcement against private holders was uneven and limited. Fewer than one third of Americans are estimated to have surrendered their gold voluntarily. The majority simply retained it. In most cases, nothing happened.

In 1974, Americans were once again permitted to own gold legally. Those who patiently held their gold during the intervening years emerged on the other side with their wealth intact. Unjust laws are often reversed.

This is the primary defense against state seizure: hold your own keys.

Bitcoin held with so-called trusted third parties can be frozen, seized, or surrendered without your consent. Bitcoin held in self-custody cannot be taken automatically.

Discretion also matters. During the gold confiscation era, the small number of private citizens who were personally targeted tended to be the obvious ones. Public figures. Vocal opponents. Those who drew attention to themselves unnecessarily. Most private holders who kept a low profile were left alone.

Lastly, jurisdictions compete. If your country treats peaceful savers as criminals, relocation is a rational response. Peace of mind matters. You will sleep better where your principles are not liabilities.

9. Physical Coercion

Targeted attacks against known holders. Sometimes called a $5 Wrench Attack.

Rare, but real.

Defense:

Physical coercion relies on surprise, speed, and brute force. Defense relies on discretion, preparedness, and layered physical deterrence.

First, keep a low profile. Avoid advertising your holdings. The correct answer to *"How much Bitcoin do you have?"* is *"Not enough."* Publicizing a sizable Bitcoin stack attracts attention, and attention invites risk. No one needs to know the size of your holdings but you.

Be prepared. Avoid creating a single, easily accessible honeypot. Meaningful holdings are often spread across multiple wallets, locations, or jurisdictions for a reason. Concentration creates single points of failure.

Physical deterrence matters the most in a $5 Wrench Attack scenario. Cameras, lighting, alerts, and a barking dog increase awareness. Multiple locked barriers slow intruders. Hand-to-hand combat skills are useful, but no one can karate chop a bullet. Firearms, training, and familiarity with their use matter. Some also maintain a decoy wallet in case all these defenses are overcome.

Have someone you can call besides the police. Response time matters.

10. Covert Theft

Someone you trusted steals your keys. Sometimes called an Evil Maid attack.

Defense:

Hidden is not secure. Drawers and closets are easily searched.

Store keys behind physical locks requiring force or specialized tools to breach. Use tamper-evident containers. Inspect regularly.

If compromise occurs, logs, cameras, and transaction monitoring can help identify the culprit. Law enforcement may then recover funds.

Do not tempt fate. Openings invite wrongdoing.

11. Overly Complex Setups

Failed multisig. Poor sharding. Self-lockout.

Defense:

Simplify. Use only what you understand fully. For most people, multi-signature introduces unnecessary failure modes, including forgotten derivation paths.

Test recovery. If something goes wrong, a trusted, technically competent Bitcoiner may be able to help you, but do not rely on rescue. Keep it simple.

Tradeoffs Are Real

Custody always involves tradeoffs.
   Self-custody removes counterparty risk and increases personal responsibility.
   Outsourced custody reduces the risk of lost keys while introducing seizure

risk.

There is no universal solution. Only conscious design.

Defense begins close to home. Secure the inner sanctum first. Then the exterior. Then the surroundings. Bitcoin rewards those who are adept at adversarial thinking.

Every citadel has its walls.

The Worst Case Scenario

At some point, nearly every Bitcoiner hears a familiar jibe from a goldbug, often delivered with snark:

"Sure, Bitcoin is great. Until the internet goes out."

This objection is usually framed as a decisive checkmate. But it rests on a misunderstanding. The internet going out does not kill Bitcoin. At most, it pauses it.

Bitcoin is not a fragile process that collapses the moment connectivity is interrupted. It is a distributed ledger with a shared history. If global connectivity were temporarily disrupted, block production would simply pause. No coins would be lost. No balances would change. Nothing would be erased.

When connectivity returns, even partially, nodes would reconnect, reconcile, and continue producing blocks exactly where they left off.

It is also difficult to imagine a scenario in which all internet connectivity across the entire planet disappears simultaneously. Short of an extreme event such as a massive solar flare, outages tend to be regional and temporary. Even in a worst case Carrington Event scenario, infrastructure can be rebuilt. Cellular towers can be restored. Fiber can be relaid.

There are enough engineers alive today, and enough accumulated knowledge preserved in physical books and offline systems, that rebuilding global communication is well within human capability. The internet is infrastructure. And infrastructure can be reconstructed.

When it is, Bitcoin resumes.

The more revealing aspect of this objection emerges when it is taken to its logical extreme.

Suppose civilization truly collapsed. Not temporarily, but permanently. Suppose global communication never returned. Suppose humanity was hurled back in time technologically and the internet was gone for good.

In that world, we would not return to a gold standard.

We would be living under a lead standard.

In such conditions, gold coins offer little protection. Imagine a goldbug attempting to trade a handful of coins with a local warlord for cans of beans. Unless that goldbug is also heavily armed and has ample backup, that transaction is unlikely to end well for him.

When civilization collapses completely, money yields to power.

Therefore, to be more bullish on gold than Bitcoin is to be unrealistically pessimistic about the future of humanity. To be bullish on Bitcoin is to be rightfully bullish on the indomitable human spirit, even (especially) after the inevitable collapse of fiat.

The closest historical analogue to the collapse of a modern fiat empire is the end of the Roman Empire. Monetary debasement, declining institutional capacity, and loss of loyalty to Rome reached a tipping point. Nobody was willing to fight and die for Rome anymore, though many were still willing to fight for their family, their local town, and Christendom. Power balkanized. Fiefdoms absorbed the power vacuum. Some of these had just rulers who defended and treated their subjects well. Others had oppressive tyrants, or were entirely bereft of leadership, and were ransacked by invaders.

Civilization did not collapse. It transformed.

Bitcoin is often said to be money for your enemies. By its neutral nature, the best game-theoretic move in a world where Bitcoin exists is to acquire some, even if you doubt it. For this reason, Bitcoin is the ideal asset to hold during the next great civilizational transition.

The Inner Shift

Something changes when you take defense seriously.

You move differently through the world. You pay attention. You plan ahead. You think in layers. You become harder to rush, harder to manipulate, harder to corner. You feel more grounded, more capable, more self-sufficient.

When you are responsible for your own security, you stop outsourcing your sense of safety entirely to distant institutions. You still value help. You still cooperate. You still rely on others when it is wise to do so. But the center of gravity moves inward. You become steadier.

This has second-order effects. A person who is calm, prepared, and alert contributes to the safety of those around them. A household that is well

DEFENSE

secured makes a neighborhood safer. A community of people who take responsibility for themselves deters opportunistic harm.

Attackers seek softness. Easy targets. A composed, capable individual is not an easy target.

This is one of Bitcoin's subtler ripple effects. It encourages people to become pillars rather than liabilities. To stabilize rather than outsource. You move from the fiat habit of assuming someone else will handle it to the adult posture of handling what is yours.

And in doing so, you make the world around you a little more secure.

18

Religion

"Thou art That."
— Uddālaka Āruṇi, Chāndogya Upanishad (circa 800 BC)

Theists and Atheists

Bitcoin does not answer religious questions, but it reliably leads people to ask them.

This is a natural consequence of following The Way. When money no longer demands constant attention, deeper questions surface. Questions about meaning, responsibility, suffering, and how to live well. Across history, religion has been humanity's primary way of engaging with these questions, even as modern culture often dismisses it.

What is reality? What is my place within it?

Some prefer to use the word God to describe the totality of existence. Others prefer the less loaded, more scientific term, cosmos. In many cases, these are synonyms for the same thing. The difference is often semantic rather than a true opposition of views.

I remember once, in university, a professor told us a story about his life.

He had grown up an atheist, convinced that believers were credulous, simple-minded naïves. Then his brother died in a car crash. Through his suffering, he found God.

When I heard him say this, I scoffed. I was a staunch atheist at the time, though I was raised Catholic in childhood. He noticed. He looked directly at me. Not with judgment. Not with scorn. But with understanding. As if he were looking at a past version of himself.

I remember thinking he had let emotion overwhelm reason. That grief had compromised his rationality. Who could believe in something as ridiculous as a sky daddy, a Santa Claus figure in the clouds, always watching, knowing everything, yet nowhere to be found when you actually look at the world?

God Within

Later in life, something shifted.

I began exploring Eastern traditions, largely through the work of Alan Watts. This opened an entirely different frame, and helped me appreciate Catholicism itself in a new light.

God is not something out there, seated on a throne, watching and judging from afar.

God is in here.

In the heart. In the mind. In consciousness itself.

The Mahayana Buddhists understand this. Jesus understands this. Every enlightened being, across traditions, comes to understand this.

> *"You are an aperture through which the universe looks at itself."*
> – Alan Watts, Out of Your Mind lecture (late 1960s)

One reason Bitcoin can help unlock this realization is subtle but profound.

When you join Bitcoin, you join a network. You are one node among many. And yet, if you run your own node, you also contain the entire timechain within you.

You are a part of the whole, and the whole is present within the part.

Indra's Net

This mirrors how Hindu theology describes reality through the metaphor of Indra's Net:

> *"Imagine, at dawn, a multidimensional spider's web covered in dew: a vast, vast spider's web that is the whole cosmos, not merely a flat thing, but a structure extending in many dimensions, covered with jewels of dew, each reflecting all the others. Every drop contains the reflection of every other drop. And within each reflection are all the others again, ad infinitum."*
> — Alan Watts, Religion of No Religion lecture (1965)

RELIGION

When you come to accept that you are not separate from the universe, but an expression of it. That you are made of the same stardust as everything else. That matter and energy are neither created nor destroyed, only transformed. Something changes.

You feel less alone, because you realize you never were. You carry God within you.

This realization provides immense inner strength. Read the accounts of Christian martyrs and you will see the extraordinary burdens humans can bear when they recognize this source within themselves.

If the word God still feels too loaded, think of it as the strength of the cosmos within you.

The substance is the same. You are made of the same stuff that fills the universe. And being conscious yourself, why would you assume the universe is not also conscious?

Tat Tvam Asi. Thou art That.

19

Governance

> "Unless... either philosophers become kings in our states or those whom we now call our kings and rulers take to the pursuit of philosophy seriously and adequately, and there is a conjunction of these two things, political power and philosophic intelligence, while the motley horde of the natures who at present pursue either apart from the other are compulsorily excluded, there can be no cessation of troubles... for our states, nor... for the human race either."
> — Plato, The Republic (circa 375 BC)

Bitcoiners often experience internal political changes when they follow The Way.

Whatever your politics may have been beforehand, a pattern emerges. First, you tend to shift toward more libertarian views.

This emerges from a desire to be left alone. To operate as a sovereign individual who holds his own keys. To live and let live, without the state interfering. This mindset has its place.

But as Bitcoiners go further down the path, another realization appears.

No man is truly a sovereign individual. No man is an island.

You may believe you have everything handled personally. But if your streets become unsafe, if your neighborhood deteriorates, if the rule of law collapses, you alone will not be able to restore order. Coordinated action is required. Authority, structure, and enforcement are unavoidable realities of human life.

Because of this, many Bitcoiners then move from libertarianism toward something more grounded: a desire for competent leadership.

The man who only wants to be left alone tends to lose to the man who wants to rule. As Plato observed, *"One of the penalties for refusing to participate in politics is that you end up being governed by your inferiors."*

For Bitcoin to maximally succeed over the long term, it helps to have Bitcoiners in positions of political power. There are no magic islands we can retreat to and live out pure libertarian dreams. There are only nation-states, connected to other nation-states. With strengths. Weaknesses. Resources. Trade agreements. Disputes.

This is the world as it is.

Reality must be accepted before it can be steered in a more fruitful direction.

Curtis Yarvin has described this moment as taking the clear pill. When this happens, institutions are no longer viewed through reverence or outrage, but as systems shaped by incentives, populated by ordinary humans, capable of both order and failure.

Another realization often follows, especially when one studies history.

Governance is cyclical.

Systems of governance are not static. They rise, harden, decay, and are replaced. This has happened in every civilization, under every form of rule.

The lesson is not to worship any particular system, but to recognize when one is healthy, when it is failing, and what kind of leadership a given moment requires.

Bitcoin is more robust, more decentralized, and harder to change than any human political institution. But it is not effortless, and it is not automatic.

If you choose not to run a node, you are relying on other people's nodes. You are deferring responsibility. This is not necessarily a moral failure. Not everyone is called to run a node. Not everyone is called to participate in high-level technical discourse or review the latest Bitcoin Improvement Proposals.

But if you *are* capable. If you *are* technically inclined. If you *do* understand the system well enough to contribute. Then foregoing what you are called on to do *is* irresponsible.

Bitcoin remains sovereign because enough people choose to bear responsibility rather than outsource it. Governance does not disappear. It is maintained by the people who show up.

Plato understood that justice in the state mirrors justice in the soul.

Philosopher-kings are those who cultivate wisdom, discipline, and restraint within themselves before exercising authority over others.

They serve something higher than their own ego.

20

Dynasty

"A good man leaveth an inheritance to his children's children."
— Proverbs 13:22, King James Version (1611)

Dynastic thinking begins when time stretches beyond the individual.

Under the gold standard, this was commonplace. Aristocratic families would hand down land, treasure, and titles to their heirs, often with centuries of continuity. But in the fiat era, the rule is *"Rags to riches to rags in three generations."* Why?

The answer is fiat inflation. Even at 2% inflation per year, which is far lower than real inflation and the stated goal of most fiat-era governments, money loses half its purchasing power every 50 years. This does not even account for confiscatory tax policies. No wonder it feels as if every generation must start from scratch. Hardly anything is left at the end of a hard-working, productive life post-1971.

The good news is that there is a way out. The way out is through Bitcoin.

Bitcoin represents a return to dynastic thinking.

There will never be more than twenty-one million Bitcoin. That fact alone alters how the future is perceived. What is scarce today will be scarcer tomorrow. What is secured now will matter more later. Time begins to feel continuous rather than fragmented when you think in terms of the Bitcoin timechain.

For those with children, this realization lands with force. It has become a meme among Bitcoiners to imagine their grandchildren with a portrait of the first Bitcoiner in the family, the one who was able not only to stack a whole coin during his lifetime, but to bestow it upon his descendants. This is how dynasties are formed. And it is, in many ways, superior to land: harder to tax, easier to transport, scarcer, and less subject to seizure.

Even if you are only able to pass down 0.1 Bitcoin, or some smaller amount, this may become immensely meaningful one or two generations from now, given Bitcoin's fixed supply and the compounding effects of the halving. Every bit counts.

Another reason leaving an inheritance in Bitcoin is likely to exceed expectations has to do with artificial intelligence.

As AI and robotics advance, the relative ability of people to earn a living through labor alone diminishes. It will never disappear entirely. Some work will always be better performed by humans. But many jobs people grind through today will vanish tomorrow.

As the leverage of labor declines, the leverage of scarce capital increases.

Consider how much can already be accomplished with 0.001 BTC worth of compute. Now imagine what will be possible as AI and robotics grow more capable and efficient. Unlike other assets whose supply increases as price rises, Bitcoin's supply cannot expand in response to demand. When gold rises in price, more gold mines open. When Bitcoin rises in price, nothing changes. The supply is fixed, forever.

By leaving Bitcoin to your heirs, you give them freedom, choices, and optionality. You give them a buffer against uncertainty in a world of accelerating technological change and narrowing traditional paths to stability.

Of course, heirs may squander their inheritance. But it is also possible to structure access so that only a portion unlocks per generation. And even if it is squandered, they had the chance. They were given a head start to live life on their own terms. That alone is an immense gift.

For those without children, or those who do not plan to have them, dynastic thinking can still apply.

You may choose to build a memetic rather than a genetic dynasty. You could create a foundation, as Ram Dass did with his *Love Serve Remember Foundation*, carrying forward what you find most meaningful long after you are gone.

The Old Norse understood this well. As the *Poetic Edda* reminds us:

> "Cattle die, kinsmen die,
>   you yourself will die;
>   one thing I know that never dies:
>   the reputation of each dead man."
>   — Hávamál, Poetic Edda (circa 1270 AD)

Others feel a kinship not with descendants, but with fellow Bitcoiners. Some have publicly stated that upon their death, they intend to let their Bitcoin die with them, effectively donating value to every remaining holder by reducing the circulating supply.

Some even do this while alive by intentionally sending small amounts of Bitcoin to provably lost addresses, including those associated with Satoshi. It is like tossing a coin into a wishing well, except the benefit is shared by everyone.

Satoshi himself acknowledged this dynamic:

> *"Lost coins only make everyone else's coins worth slightly more. Think of it as a donation to everyone."*
> — Satoshi Nakamoto, BitcoinTalk forum (2010)

Do what feels right to you.

And be mindful of death. It comes for us all. Better to plan your inheritance deliberately than to leave it to chance or allow the kleptocrats to seize it.

Memento mori.

21

The Raft

"When you cross a river on a raft and you get to the other shore, you do not pick up the raft and carry it on your back."
— Alan Watts, Buddhism: The Religion of No Religion (1965)

The Buddha described his teaching as a raft.

You board a raft because you need it to cross a river. You use it. You rely on it. And when you reach the other shore, you step off. You do not pick it up and carry it with you forever.

Bitcoin works in the same way.

At first, The Way of Bitcoin appears urgent. You study it. You think about it constantly. You reorganize your habits around it. You realize that money is stored time, and that how you save shapes how you live.

For a period, Bitcoin stands in the foreground. But tools are not meant to be clung to.

Once The Way of Bitcoin is fully integrated, it recedes. It becomes habit. It becomes ordinary. Saving no longer requires vigilance. Work proceeds without constant anxiety about the future. Planning resumes on solid ground.

Nothing dramatic happens. And yet life stabilizes. This is how you know the raft has done its job.

There is a temptation, once you have crossed the river, to turn back and shout instructions. To urge others to hurry. To feel frustration toward those still standing on the bank, or paddling their rafts in circles. This too is a way of carrying the raft on your back.

G. K. Chesterton once wrote, *"Angels can fly because they take themselves lightly."*

The aim is not to become heavy with certainty or judgment. The aim is lightness.

Alan Watts put it this way:

> *"If you really see into this secret, that the world doesn't contain any serious threats because it's all the basic you running up behind itself and saying boo to see if you can get yourself to jump out of your skin, then be cool. That's the whole art of Zen."*
> — Alan Watts, Face Your Problems Head-On (1971)

Be cool. Save in Bitcoin. Focus on your craft. Live a peaceful life.

If the contents of this book ever felt overwhelming, that is natural. The Way becomes easier the further you walk it. It takes time for habits, expectations, and rhythms to adjust. Once they do, effort fades into routine.

Any sufficiently advanced technology disappears. Bitcoin follows the same pattern.

Today it may appear novel. Tomorrow it becomes commonplace. Bitcoin will one day no longer be thought of as magic internet money. It will simply be money. You earn it through your work. You save it. You spend it when needed. You pass it on when the time comes. Much like under the gold standard, but updated for a digital world.

And when this becomes natural, you move on. Satoshi himself moved on.

> *"I've moved on to other things."*
> — Satoshi Nakamoto, private email to Mike Hearn (2011)

Some speculate this was for health reasons, or for operational security, or because it was what the network needed in order to mature without a central figure.

There may be truth in all of these explanations.

It may also be that he was simply ready to move on.

Bitcoin will always require stewards, so moving on does not mean abandoning responsibility. It does not mean stopping your node, ceasing to save, or refusing to speak when asked. It means Bitcoin no longer occupies the center of your attention. And one day, even stewardship may loosen its grip. You will know when.

The Way is not something you carry. It is something you walk.

Others will find it when they are ready.

Appendix A: A Brief History of Money

Reputation as Social Currency (Prehistory to circa 4,500 BC)

Before money, there was reputation.

Picture your hunter-gatherer ancestors tens of thousands of years ago.

They move across open land, living by the hunt and by the seasons. Everyone knows who can be relied upon and who cannot. Reputation travels, even when people are far apart. A person's standing is built slowly, through repeated acts, witnessed and remembered.

Among family, resources are shared as a matter of belonging. Beyond family, resources are shared based on mutual understanding.

Hunters range far. Some days they return empty-handed. Other days they bring down more than they can consume alone. A mammoth feeds many.

Nearby, women gather berries, roots, and edible plants. Their work is steady and essential. When game runs thin, their knowledge of the land sustains the group. Their contribution is visible. Their reliability is known.

As bands encounter other bands, kinship no longer binds behavior. Trust must be earned. Some neighboring clans share freely when their hunt succeeds and offer shelter when storms come early. Their actions are remembered. When scarcity arrives, they are included.

Other clans behave differently. They take but do not return. They share only when pressed. Their reputation spreads just as quickly. When resources grow scarce, they find doors closed and fires unlit.

Reputation becomes a form of currency. It travels between groups. It determines who trades, who eats, and who survives.

This is the earliest form of money beyond kinship. A social ledger enforced by honor, memory, and consequence.

Barter and Its Limits (circa 4,500 BC to 3,000 BC)

As communities grow larger and more specialized, barter emerges. One person has grain. Another has tools. A third has livestock. Exchange becomes direct and explicit.

Barter works at small scale, yet it carries friction. Each trade requires a coincidence of wants. The grain farmer must want tools at the same moment the toolmaker wants grain. Many potential trades never occur because timing and needs fail to align.

Barter also struggles across distance and time. Some goods spoil. Others remain bulky or difficult to divide. Value becomes hard to compare. A goat today differs from a goat tomorrow. Negotiation consumes effort that could be spent producing.

As trade expands beyond neighbors and familiar faces, barter slows coordination. It limits specialization. It constrains growth.

Money emerges as a shared language of value. It allows indirect exchange. A farmer sells grain for money. That money is later used to acquire tools, labor, or land. Trade decouples. Markets deepen. Productivity rises.

The choice of money matters. Over time, societies that adopt scarce, durable forms of money coordinate more effectively than those that do not.

Gold and the Long Arc of Value (circa 4,500 BC to 1600 AD)

As generations pass, villages form and trade networks widen. Reputation and barter alone struggle to carry trust far enough.

Communities experiment with a variety of objects as money. Over time, one material proves uniquely suited to the task.

Gold first enters human awareness through beauty. A gleam in a riverbed. A metal that holds light. It is collected, admired, and kept.

Over time, gold becomes adornment. A necklace worn by a lover. An arm ring worn by a warrior. Something held close, given meaning through craftsmanship and symbolism.

Then another shift occurs. Gold outlasts the people who hold it. It survives fire, flood, and war. A ring passes from parent to child. Gold becomes a vessel for continuity, capable of carrying value forward through generations.

As exchange expands, gold's durability, divisibility, and relative scarcity allow it to circulate reliably. Coinage standardizes weight and purity. Value becomes legible. Other goods begin to be measured against this common standard.

For everyday transactions, less valuable metals circulate alongside gold, such as silver and copper, allowing trade to function at different scales. Gold remains the reference point.

Once established, societies that standardize and protect their coinage gain a decisive advantage.

In Classical Greece, Athens issues silver drachmae struck from the rich Laurion mines. The coins are highly consistent in weight and purity, and over time they become widely trusted across the Mediterranean. Merchants prefer them. Soldiers accept them. Tribute within the Athenian sphere increasingly flows in Athenian coin.

Nearby, the island of Aegina had earlier prospered as a maritime trading hub and was among the first Greek poleis to issue silver coinage. These coins circulated broadly in earlier periods, but their weight and purity were less consistent.

As Athenian coinage proved more uniform and reliable, merchants increasingly preferred it, and settlement converged on Athenian silver. After a series of conflicts, Athens defeated Aegina, curtailed its autonomy, and absorbed it into the Athenian empire. Monetary credibility, reinforced by naval power, translated into political dominance.

Later, Rome follows a similar path with the denarius. As long as its coinage retains integrity, Roman trade expands, taxes flow, and legions are paid. As debasement accelerates, trust erodes, economic stress mounts, and coordination breaks down.

Empires rise and fall. Gold endures. Its supply grows slowly and predictably. Over very long spans of time, a fixed quantity of gold has tended to command roughly similar amounts of skilled labor or high-quality goods.

Gold remains the soundest analog asset in existence.

Globalization and Gold Abstractions (1600 to 1913)

As trade stretches across regions and seas, carrying physical gold becomes costly and dangerous. Distance introduces friction. Risk accumulates.

To solve this, societies add layers.

Gold is stored in vaults. Paper claims circulate in its place. These claims begin as direct representations. They offer convenience while remaining grounded in physical reserves.

Layering allows trade to expand. Markets deepen. Communication accelerates. Transactions move faster than physical settlement.

As a result, credit becomes more widespread than base money, and seigniorage grants issuers first access to new purchasing power, an effect later dubbed the Cantillon Effect.

Over time, the paper layer grows larger than the metal beneath it. Trust shifts from substance to institutions.

The Early Fiat Era (1600 to 1971)

As monetary systems scale, currency becomes increasingly abstract. Gold and silver fade from daily use. Paper and later digital balances take their place.

Across history, different currencies rise to global prominence, each reflecting the productive and financial center of its era.

In the seventeenth century, the Dutch guilder dominates global trade. The

Dutch Republic builds deep capital markets, reliable accounting, maritime supremacy, and disciplined monetary practices. The guilder's credibility rests on trade, restraint, and economic might.

As financial leadership shifts, the British pound sterling assumes this role. Britain formalizes a gold-based monetary system, enforces convertibility, and supports it with industrial output, global shipping, and imperial reach. London becomes the world's financial hub.

In the twentieth century, the US dollar inherits global dominance. The United States emerges from two world wars with unmatched productive capacity, deep capital markets, and the world's largest gold reserves. The dollar anchors the Bretton Woods system and becomes the settlement currency for global trade.

Each dominant currency follows a similar path. Sound money and a robust economic foundation underwrite expansion. Layers accumulate. Credit grows. Over time, abstraction increases and claims multiply beyond underlying reserves.

As confidence weakens, dominance fades. Another system rises to take its place.

In 1913, the Federal Reserve is created, transferring monetary authority from markets to a centralized institution with the power to expand credit and adjust interest rates at will. This shift enables a banking system increasingly insulated from free market forces, encouraging leverage, moral hazard, and the compounding buildup of unsound debt.

Rather than preventing crises, central banking amplifies them. Artificial credit expansion fuels booms. Contraction follows. During the Great Depression, policy errors deepen the collapse by distorting price signals, misallocating capital, and undermining trust in money.

In 1933, Executive Order 6102 forbids most Americans from holding gold, as a way of preventing an exit from the dollar system. Private ownership remains restricted until 1975.

In 1971, the final link is severed. The US dollar floats freely as President Nixon ends its convertibility to gold. Money becomes fiat. Its stability rests on policy and enforcement.

The world has grown vast and fast. Organic systems strain under the load.

The Late-Stage Fiat Era (1971 to 2008)

Computers shrink. Networks spread. The internet connects the world.

Capital moves at extraordinary speed. Settlement lags behind. Credit expands rapidly. Financial instruments multiply. Leverage becomes systemic.

Markets grow larger, more complex, and increasingly fragile. Debt compounds faster than productive output. Risk concentrates within opaque institutions.

When failure arrives, government bailouts follow. Losses are socialized. Confidence thins.

By the early 2000s, deep cracks become visible. Asset bubbles inflate and burst. Imbalances grow harder to conceal. The Great Recession of 2008 exposes the structural weakness of a system built on layered promises rather than solid foundations.

The Chancellor is on the brink of yet another bailout for banks, a moment later immortalized in the Bitcoin Genesis Block.

The modern fiat system shows signs of exhaustion. A digital world demands a form of money that settles as fast as information, yet is also scarce, verifiable, and internet native.

The Bitcoin Era (2008 to Present)

Out of this landscape, something old returns in a new form. Bitcoin.

For the first time, scarcity exists in the digital realm. A ledger open to inspection. Rules enforced by consensus rather than decree. Settlement without trusted third parties. Triple entry accounting. Magic internet money. Digital gold.

The Bitcoin Whitepaper publishes on October 31st, 2008, to the Cryptography Mailing List.

On January 3rd, 2009, the Genesis Block is mined. For the first week or so, Satoshi Nakamoto is the only known miner, securing the system alone while validating its behavior under real world conditions.

On January 10th, 2009, Hal Finney downloads the software and begins running Bitcoin, becoming the first known participant besides Satoshi to do so. Two days later, Satoshi sends Hal the first recorded Bitcoin transaction, marking the transition from a solitary experiment to a shared system.

Soon after, a small group of cryptographers, cypherpunks, and techno-libertarians begin running nodes and mining Bitcoin on personal computers. There is no established price. Adoption is driven by curiosity, conviction, and interest rather than profit. The network grows participant by participant, without promotion, funding, or institutional backing.

By late 2009, BitcoinTalk becomes the primary forum for discussing Bitcoin.

In 2010, a Bitcoiner named Laszlo Hanyecz exchanges ten thousand Bitcoin for two pizzas, marking the first recorded use of Bitcoin as a medium of exchange.

Soon after, WikiLeaks begins accepting Bitcoin when cut off from traditional payment rails, thus kicking the hornet's nest. Bitcoin demonstrates censorship resistance in practice.

In 2011, Satoshi Nakamoto sends his final message and disappears. His creation remains.

Silk Road follows. Controversial yet instructive. Bitcoin functions under pressure. The marketplace is shut down in 2013. Bitcoin continues.

Hardware wallets emerge beginning in 2014. Self custody becomes practical at scale.

Exchanges expand access, making it easier to acquire Bitcoin. Custodial failures follow. Mt. Gox collapses. Bitcoin is declared dead by all but its most fervent supporters. The *not your keys, not your coins* lesson repeats across later cycles.

In 2015, the Lightning Network is proposed as a second layer scaling solution for fast, low cost Bitcoin payments. Over the years that follow, it gradually comes online, enabling near instant settlement for everyday use.

The altcoin speculative craze arrives soon thereafter. Thousands of developers fork Bitcoin's code to create new cryptocurrencies. These sacrifice decentralization, security, or monetary discipline. The vast majority fail to retain long term value. Bitcoin strengthens.

In 2017, a new wave of copycat tokens emerges during the Initial Coin Offering boom. *Blockchain not Bitcoin* becomes the motto among venture capitalists. The boom quickly turns to bust as many projects are revealed to be little more than fundraising schemes.

Later that year, the Federal Reserve shifts from a policy of Quantitative Easing to Quantitative Tightening for the first time in Bitcoin's history, responding to inflation concerns. So-called risk assets collapse in value. Many once again declare Bitcoin dead.

In 2020, the COVID shutdown heightens volatility. Markets crash. Then liquidity is injected at an unprecedented scale. Bitcoin recovers sharply, then soars to new highs. Its monetary properties draw renewed attention.

In 2021, China bans Bitcoin mining. The network's hash rate falls precipitously, then recovers steadily as miners relocate worldwide. Difficulty adjusts. Bitcoin persists.

That same year, El Salvador adopts Bitcoin as legal tender. Grassroots Bitcoin economies begin forming organically. Bitcoin Jungle. Bitcoin Park. Madeira. Bhutan begins mining Bitcoin using surplus energy. These countries gain an edge over those that ignore Bitcoin.

And yet, not everyone is convinced. Elon Musk reverses his support for Bitcoin due to stated environmental concerns, supporting a dog-themed token with an infinite supply instead. It peaks in value during his SNL appearance, then crashes. A new bear market begins.

In 2022, FTX collapses. The bear market deepens. Many declare Bitcoin dead yet again.

However, the Bitcoin price begins to recover just a few months later. Institutional participation increases. Spot Bitcoin exchange traded funds (ETFs) are approved in the United States in 2024, expanding access through traditional financial channels.

Public companies begin holding Bitcoin as a treasury asset. Nation states explore mining and accumulation strategies. Bitcoin achieves six figure dollar valuation for the first time.

Political hostility towards Bitcoiners starts to recede. In 2025, Silk Road founder Ross Ulbricht is freed from prison, and operation Choke Point 2.0 ends. Though not everyone in government is on the same page. Some open source developers continue to be prosecuted.

Bitcoin begins to enter the mainstream. And yet, it is still early.

The last of the twenty-one million Bitcoin supply will not be issued until around 2140 AD.

Appendix B: The Bitcoin Whitepaper

Below is the Bitcoin Whitepaper, reproduced verbatim as published on October 31st, 2008. Formatting adapted for print.

The paper was released by the pseudonymous creator of Bitcoin, **Satoshi Nakamoto**, via the Cryptography Mailing List.

* * *

Bitcoin: A Peer-to-Peer Electronic Cash System

Satoshi Nakamoto
satoshin@gmx.com
www.bitcoin.org

Abstract. A purely peer-to-peer version of electronic cash would allow online payments to be sent directly from one party to another without going through a financial institution. Digital signatures provide part of the solution, but the main benefits are lost if a trusted third party is still required to prevent double-spending. We propose a solution to the double-spending problem using a peer-to-peer network. The network timestamps transactions by hashing them into an ongoing chain of hash-based proof-of-work, forming a record that cannot be changed without redoing the proof-of-work. The longest chain not only serves as proof of the sequence of events witnessed, but proof that it came from the largest pool of CPU power. As long as a majority of CPU power is controlled by nodes that are not cooperating to attack the network, they'll generate the longest chain and outpace attackers. The network itself requires minimal structure. Messages are broadcast on a best effort basis, and nodes can leave and rejoin the network at will, accepting the longest proof-of-work chain as proof of what happened while they were gone.

1. Introduction

Commerce on the Internet has come to rely almost exclusively on financial institutions serving as trusted third parties to process electronic payments. While the system works well enough for most transactions, it still suffers from the inherent weaknesses of the trust based model. Completely non-reversible transactions are not really possible, since financial institutions cannot avoid mediating disputes. The cost of mediation increases transaction costs, limiting the minimum practical transaction size and cutting off the possibility for small casual transactions, and there is a broader cost in the loss of ability to make non-reversible payments for non-reversible services. With the possibility of reversal, the need for trust spreads. Merchants must be wary of their customers, hassling them for more information than they would otherwise need. A certain percentage of fraud is accepted as unavoidable. These costs and payment uncertainties can be avoided in person by using physical currency, but no mechanism exists to make payments over a communications channel without a trusted party. What is needed is an electronic payment system based on cryptographic proof instead of trust, allowing any two willing parties to transact directly with each other without the need for a trusted third party. Transactions that are computationally impractical to reverse would protect sellers from fraud, and routine escrow mechanisms could easily be implemented to protect buyers. In this paper, we propose a solution to the double-spending problem using a peer-to-peer distributed timestamp server to generate computational proof of the chronological order of transactions. The system is secure as long as honest nodes collectively control more CPU power than any cooperating group of attacker nodes.

2. Transactions

We define an electronic coin as a chain of digital signatures. Each owner transfers the coin to the next by digitally signing a hash of the previous transaction and the public key of the next owner and adding these to the end of the coin. A payee can verify the signatures to verify the chain of ownership.

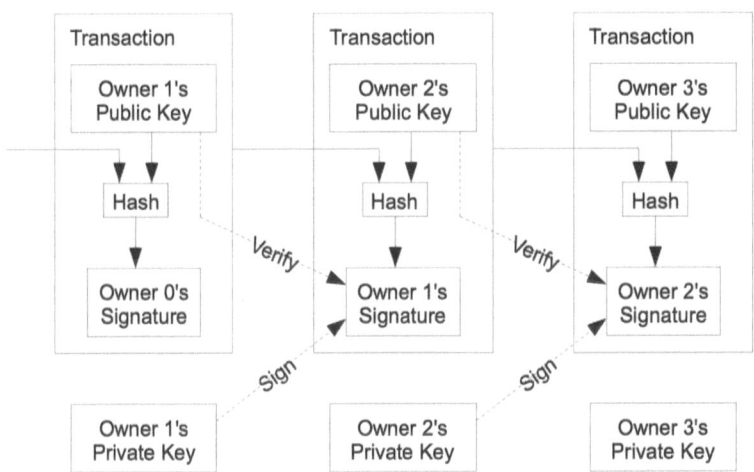

The problem of course is the payee can't verify that one of the owners did not double-spend the coin. A common solution is to introduce a trusted central authority, or mint, that checks every transaction for double spending. After each transaction, the coin must be returned to the mint to issue a new coin, and only coins issued directly from the mint are trusted not to be double-spent. The problem with this solution is that the fate of the entire money system depends on the company running the mint, with every transaction having to go through them, just like a bank. We need a way for the payee to know that the previous owners did not sign any earlier transactions. For our purposes, the earliest transaction is the one that counts, so we don't care about later attempts to double-spend. The only way to confirm the absence of a transaction is to be aware of all transactions. In the mint based model, the mint was aware of all transactions and decided which arrived first. To accomplish this without a trusted party, transactions must be publicly announced [1], and we need a system for participants to agree on a single history of the order in which they were received. The payee needs proof that at the time of each transaction, the majority of nodes agreed it was the first received.

3. Timestamp Server

The solution we propose begins with a timestamp server. A timestamp server works by taking a hash of a block of items to be timestamped and widely publishing the hash, such as in a newspaper or Usenet post [2-5]. The timestamp proves that the data must have existed at the time, obviously, in order to get into the hash. Each timestamp includes the previous timestamp in its hash, forming a chain, with each additional timestamp reinforcing the ones before it.

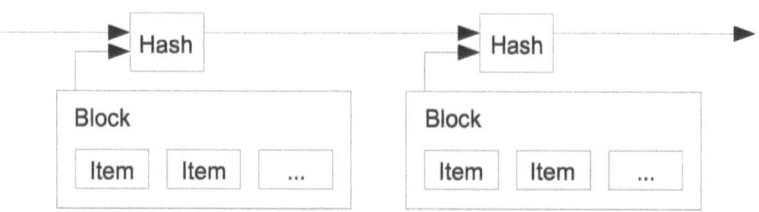

4. Proof-of-Work

To implement a distributed timestamp server on a peer-to-peer basis, we will need to use a proof-of-work system similar to Adam Back's Hashcash [6], rather than newspaper or Usenet posts. The proof-of-work involves scanning for a value that when hashed, such as with SHA-256, the hash begins with a number of zero bits. The average work required is exponential in the number of zero bits required and can be verified by executing a single hash. For our timestamp network, we implement the proof-of-work by incrementing a nonce in the block until a value is found that gives the block's hash the required zero bits. Once the CPU effort has been expended to make it satisfy the proof-of-work, the block cannot be changed without redoing the work. As later blocks are chained after it, the work to change the block would include redoing all the blocks after it.

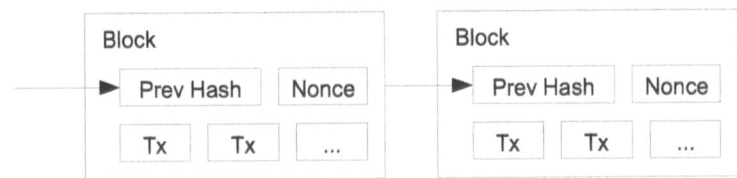

The proof-of-work also solves the problem of determining representation in majority decision making. If the majority were based on one-IP-address-one-vote, it could be subverted by anyone able to allocate many IPs. Proof-of-work is essentially one-CPU-one-vote. The majority decision is represented by the longest chain, which has the greatest proof-of-work effort invested in it. If a majority of CPU power is controlled by honest nodes, the honest chain will grow the fastest and outpace any competing chains. To modify a past block, an attacker would have to redo the proof-of-work of the block and all blocks after it and then catch up with and surpass the work of the honest nodes. We will show later that the probability of a slower attacker catching up diminishes exponentially as subsequent blocks are added. To compensate for increasing hardware speed and varying interest in running nodes over time, the proof-of-work difficulty is determined by a moving average targeting an average number of blocks per hour. If they're generated too fast, the difficulty increases.

5. Network

The steps to run the network are as follows:

1. New transactions are broadcast to all nodes.
2. Each node collects new transactions into a block.
3. Each node works on finding a difficult proof-of-work for its block.
4. When a node finds a proof-of-work, it broadcasts the block to all nodes.
5. Nodes accept the block only if all transactions in it are valid and not already spent.
6. Nodes express their acceptance of the block by working on creating the next block in the chain, using the hash of the accepted block as the previous hash.

Nodes always consider the longest chain to be the correct one and will keep working on extending it. If two nodes broadcast different versions of the next block simultaneously, some nodes may receive one or the other first. In that case, they work on the first one they received, but save the other branch in case it becomes longer. The tie will be broken when the next proof-of-work is found and one branch becomes longer; the nodes that were working on the other branch will then switch to the longer one.

New transaction broadcasts do not necessarily need to reach all nodes. As long as they reach many nodes, they will get into a block before long. Block broadcasts are also tolerant of dropped messages. If a node does not receive a block, it will request it when it receives the next block and realizes it missed one.

6. Incentive

By convention, the first transaction in a block is a special transaction that starts a new coin owned by the creator of the block. This adds an incentive for nodes to support the network, and provides a way to initially distribute coins into circulation, since there is no central authority to issue them. The steady addition of a constant amount of new coins is analogous to gold miners expending resources to add gold to circulation. In our case, it is CPU time and electricity that is expended. The incentive can also be funded with transaction fees. If the output value of a transaction is less than its input value, the difference is a transaction fee that is added to the incentive value of the block containing the transaction. Once a predetermined number of coins have entered circulation, the incentive can transition entirely to transaction fees and be completely inflation free.

The incentive may help encourage nodes to stay honest. If a greedy attacker is able to assemble more CPU power than all the honest nodes, he would have to choose between using it to defraud people by stealing back his payments, or using it to generate new coins. He ought to find it more profitable to play by the rules, such rules that favour him with more new coins than everyone else combined, than to undermine the system and the validity of his own wealth.

7. Reclaiming Disk Space

Once the latest transaction in a coin is buried under enough blocks, the spent transactions before it can be discarded to save disk space. To facilitate this without breaking the block's hash, transactions are hashed in a Merkle Tree [7][2][5], with only the root included in the block's hash. Old blocks can then be compacted by stubbing off branches of the tree. The interior hashes do not need to be stored.

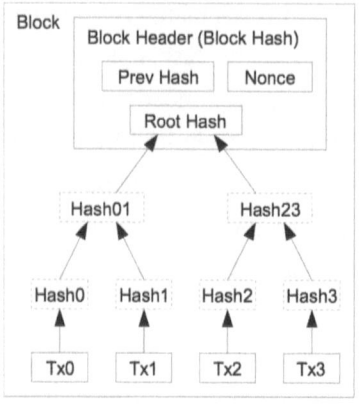 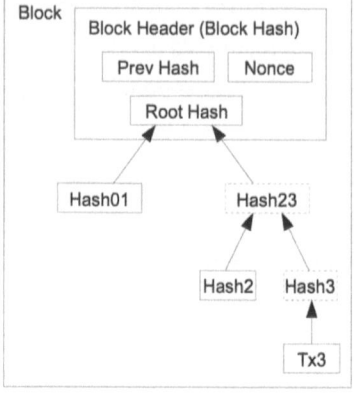

Transactions Hashed in a Merkle Tree After Pruning Tx0-2 from the Block

A block header with no transactions would be about 80 bytes. If we suppose blocks are generated every 10 minutes, 80 bytes * 6 * 24 * 365 = 4.2MB per year. With computer systems typically selling with 2GB of RAM as of 2008, and Moore's Law predicting current growth of 1.2GB per year, storage should not be a problem even if the block headers must be kept in memory.

8. Simplified Payment Verification

It is possible to verify payments without running a full network node. A user only needs to keep a copy of the block headers of the longest proof-of-work chain, which he can get by querying network nodes until he's convinced he has the longest chain, and obtain the Merkle branch linking the transaction to the block it's timestamped in. He can't check the transaction for himself, but by linking it to a place in the chain, he can see that a network node has accepted it, and blocks added after it further confirm the network has accepted it.

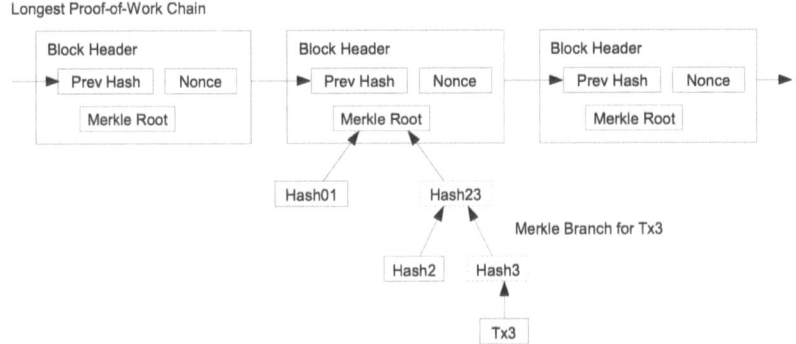

As such, the verification is reliable as long as honest nodes control the network, but is more vulnerable if the network is overpowered by an attacker. While network nodes can verify transactions for themselves, the simplified method can be fooled by an attacker's fabricated transactions for as long as the attacker can continue to overpower the network. One strategy to protect against this would be to accept alerts from network nodes when they detect an invalid block, prompting the user's software to download the full block and alerted transactions to confirm the inconsistency. Businesses that receive frequent payments will probably still want to run their own nodes for more independent security and quicker verification.

9. Combining and Splitting Value

Although it would be possible to handle coins individually, it would be unwieldy to make a separate transaction for every cent in a transfer. To allow value to be split and combined, transactions contain multiple inputs and outputs. Normally there will be either a single input from a larger previous transaction or multiple inputs combining smaller amounts, and at most two outputs: one for the payment, and one returning the change, if any, back to the sender.

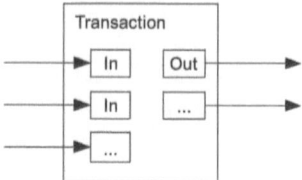

It should be noted that fan-out, where a transaction depends on several transactions, and those transactions depend on many more, is not a problem here. There is never the need to extract a complete standalone copy of a transaction's history.

10. Privacy

The traditional banking model achieves a level of privacy by limiting access to information to the parties involved and the trusted third party. The necessity to announce all transactions publicly precludes this method, but privacy can still be maintained by breaking the flow of information in another place: by keeping public keys anonymous. The public can see that someone is sending an amount to someone else, but without information linking the transaction to anyone. This is similar to the level of information released by stock exchanges, where the time and size of individual trades, the "tape", is made public, but without telling who the parties were.

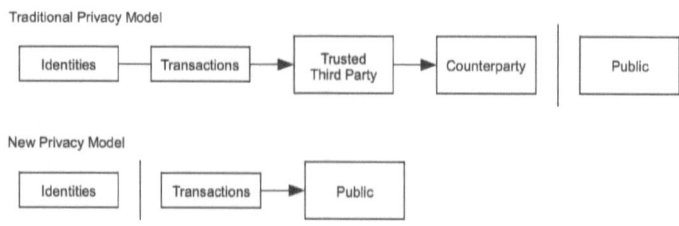

As an additional firewall, a new key pair should be used for each transaction to keep them from being linked to a common owner. Some linking is still unavoidable with multi-input transactions, which necessarily reveal that their inputs were owned by the same owner. The risk is that if the owner of a key is revealed, linking could reveal other transactions that belonged to the same owner.

11. Calculations

We consider the scenario of an attacker trying to generate an alternate chain faster than the honest chain. Even if this is accomplished, it does not throw the system open to arbitrary changes, such as creating value out of thin air or taking money that never belonged to the attacker. Nodes are not going to accept an invalid transaction as payment, and honest nodes will never accept a block containing them. An attacker can only try to change one of his own transactions to take back money he recently spent. The race between the honest chain and an attacker chain can be characterized as a Binomial Random Walk. The success event is the honest chain being extended by one block, increasing its lead by +1, and the failure event is the attacker's chain being extended by one block, reducing the gap by -1. The probability of an attacker catching up from a given deficit is analogous to a Gambler's Ruin problem. Suppose a gambler with unlimited credit starts at a deficit and plays potentially an infinite number of trials to try to reach breakeven. We can calculate the probability he ever reaches breakeven, or that an attacker ever catches up with the honest chain, as follows [8]:

- p = probability an honest node finds the next block
- q = probability the attacker finds the next block
- q_z = probability the attacker will ever catch up from z blocks behind

$$q_z = \begin{cases} 1 & \text{if } p \leq q \\ (q/p)^z & \text{if } p > q \end{cases}$$

Given our assumption that p > q, the probability drops exponentially as the number of blocks the attacker has to catch up with increases. With the odds against him, if he doesn't make a lucky lunge forward early on, his chances become vanishingly small as he falls further behind.

We now consider how long the recipient of a new transaction needs to wait before being sufficiently certain the sender can't change the transaction. We assume the sender is an attacker who wants to make the recipient believe he paid him for a while, then switch it to pay back to himself after some time has passed. The receiver will be alerted when that happens, but the sender hopes it will be too late.

The receiver generates a new key pair and gives the public key to the sender shortly before signing. This prevents the sender from preparing a chain of blocks ahead of time by working on it continuously until he is lucky enough to get far enough ahead, then executing the transaction at that moment. Once the transaction is sent, the dishonest sender starts working in secret on a parallel chain containing an alternate version of his transaction.

The recipient waits until the transaction has been added to a block and z blocks have been linked after it. He doesn't know the exact amount of progress the attacker has made, but assuming the honest blocks took the average expected time per block, the attacker's potential progress will be a Poisson distribution with expected value:

$$\lambda = z\frac{q}{p}$$

To get the probability the attacker could still catch up now, we multiply the Poisson density for each amount of progress he could have made by the probability he could catch up from that point:

$$\sum_{k=0}^{\infty} \frac{\lambda^k e^{-\lambda}}{k!} \cdot \begin{cases} (q/p)^{(z-k)} & \text{if } k \leq z \\ 1 & \text{if } k > z \end{cases}$$

Rearranging to avoid summing the infinite tail of the distribution...

$$1 - \sum_{k=0}^{z} \frac{\lambda^k e^{-\lambda}}{k!}\left(1 - (q/p)^{(z-k)}\right)$$

Converting to C code...

```
#include <math.h>
double AttackerSuccessProbability(double q, int z)
{
  double p = 1.0 - q;
  double lambda = z * (q / p);
  double sum = 1.0;
  int i, k;
  for (k = 0; k <= z; k++)
  {
    double poisson = exp(-lambda);
```

```
  for (i = 1; i <= k; i++)
  poisson *= lambda / i;
  sum -= poisson * (1 - pow(q / p, z - k));
  }
  return sum;
}
```

Running some results, we can see the probability drop off exponentially with z.

```
q=0.1
z=0   P=1.0000000
z=1   P=0.2045873
z=2   P=0.0509779
z=3   P=0.0131722
z=4   P=0.0034552
z=5   P=0.0009137
z=6   P=0.0002428
z=7   P=0.0000647
z=8   P=0.0000173
z=9   P=0.0000046
z=10  P=0.0000012
q=0.3
z=0   P=1.0000000
z=5   P=0.1773523
z=10  P=0.0416605
z=15  P=0.0101008
z=20  P=0.0024804
z=25  P=0.0006132
z=30  P=0.0001522
z=35  P=0.0000379
z=40  P=0.0000095
z=45  P=0.0000024
z=50  P=0.0000006
```

Solving for P less than 0.1%...

$P < 0.001$
$q=0.10$ $z=5$
$q=0.15$ $z=8$
$q=0.20$ $z=11$
$q=0.25$ $z=15$
$q=0.30$ $z=24$
$q=0.35$ $z=41$
$q=0.40$ $z=89$
$q=0.45$ $z=340$

12. Conclusion

We have proposed a system for electronic transactions without relying on trust. We started with the usual framework of coins made from digital signatures, which provides strong control of ownership, but is incomplete without a way to prevent double-spending. To solve this, we proposed a peer-to-peer network using proof-of-work to record a public history of transactions that quickly becomes computationally impractical for an attacker to change if honest nodes control a majority of CPU power. The network is robust in its unstructured simplicity. Nodes work all at once with little coordination. They do not need to be identified, since messages are not routed to any particular place and only need to be delivered on a best effort basis. Nodes can leave and rejoin the network at will, accepting the proof-of-work chain as proof of what happened while they were gone. They vote with their CPU power, expressing their acceptance of valid blocks by working on extending them and rejecting invalid blocks by refusing to work on them. Any needed rules and incentives can be enforced with this consensus mechanism.

References

1. W. Dai, "b-money," http://www.weidai.com/bmoney.txt, 1998.
2. H. Massias, X.S. Avila, and J.-J. Quisquater, "Design of a secure timestamping service with minimal trust requirements," In 20th Symposium

on Information Theory in the Benelux, May 1999.
3. S. Haber, W.S. Stornetta, "How to time-stamp a digital document," In Journal of Cryptology, vol 3, no 2, pages 99-111, 1991.
4. D. Bayer, S. Haber, W.S. Stornetta, "Improving the efficiency and reliability of digital time-stamping," In Sequences II: Methods in Communication, Security and Computer Science, pages 329-334, 1993.
5. S. Haber, W.S. Stornetta, "Secure names for bit-strings," In Proceedings of the 4th ACM Conference on Computer and Communications Security, pages 28-35, April 1997.
6. A. Back, "Hashcash - a denial of service counter-measure," http://www.hashcash.org/papers/hashcash.pdf, 2002.
7. R.C. Merkle, "Protocols for public key cryptosystems," In Proc. 1980 Symposium on Security and Privacy, IEEE Computer Society, pages 122-133, April 1980.
8. W. Feller, "An introduction to probability theory and its applications," 1957.

Appendix C: Further Reading

21 Lessons: What I've Learned from Falling Down the Bitcoin Rabbit Hole by Gigi
An ideal intro to Bitcoin. Clear, concise, and grounded in first principles.

The Book of Satoshi by Phil Champagne
A curated collection of Satoshi Nakamoto's writings. The primary source.

The Book: On the Taboo Against Knowing Who You Are by Alan Watts
A foundational work on Zen, identity, and the philosophy of The Way.

Glossary

Altcoin

Any cryptocurrency other than Bitcoin.

Altcoin Casino

An exchange that promotes trading in altcoins.

Bitcoin

The first and only truly decentralized digital money.

Bitcoin Maximalism

The philosophy that Bitcoin is the soundest money, destined to be the global standard.

BitcoinTalk Forum

The original online forum for discussing Bitcoin, launched in November 2009.

Blockchain

A distributed ledger that records transactions in chronological blocks, secured through cryptography and maintained by a decentralized network.

Cantillon Effect

The uneven economic effects of new money or credit entering an economy through specific channels, benefiting early recipients while disadvantaging those who receive it later.

Cold Storage

The practice of generating and storing Bitcoin private keys offline to minimize exposure.

Decoy Wallet

A wallet containing a relatively small amount of Bitcoin intended to reduce risk in the event of coercion, thus providing plausible deniability.

Difficulty Adjustment

A mechanism in Bitcoin's protocol that automatically adjusts the mining difficulty every 2,016 blocks (~2 weeks) to target an average block interval of 10 minutes.

En Passant

A rule in chess where, if a pawn moves two squares forward from its starting position and lands beside an enemy pawn, that enemy pawn may capture it on the next move as if it had moved only one square forward.

Exchange

A platform that allows users to buy, sell, or trade assets such as Bitcoin.

Fiat (General Usage)

From Latin meaning "let it be done." Used to describe systems sustained by decree rather than organic feedback, often expedient in the short run but harmful in the long run.

Fiat Money

Money deriving its value from government decree rather than organic market emergence.

F.U.D.

An acronym for fear, uncertainty, and doubt.

Genesis Block

The first block in the Bitcoin blockchain, from which all subsequent blocks descend.

God Candle

A sudden and dramatic upward price movement in Bitcoin.

HODL

A term originating from a misspelled "HOLD" online post. Used to describe the philosophy of holding Bitcoin long-term rather than trading it.

Lightning Network

A second-layer protocol built on top of Bitcoin that enables faster and lower-cost transactions by settling many payments off-chain.

Lindy Effect

The observation that the future life expectancy of a non-perishable thing tends to increase the longer it exists.

Memetic Dynasty

A legacy built through ideas, teachings, or creative works that persist across generations.

Mining

The process by which new Bitcoin are issued and transactions are secured via proof of work.

Node

A computer running Bitcoin that independently verifies transactions and enforces the rules.

Orange Pill

A metaphor describing the moment someone comes to understand Bitcoin.

OPSEC

Short for operations security. The practice of minimizing risk vectors.

Pareto Efficiency

A condition in which no change can be made to improve one aspect without worsening another.

Private Key

A cryptographic secret that grants control over Bitcoin.

Public Key

A cryptographic identifier derived from a private key, used to receive Bitcoin.

Proof-of-Work

A consensus mechanism that requires participants known as miners to expend computational energy to secure the network, making attacks costly and verifiable.

Rehypothecation

The practice of reusing collateral that has already been pledged, increasing systemic risk.

Replace-by-Fee (RBF)

A Bitcoin transaction feature that allows a sender to increase the transaction fee after broadcasting, enabling the transaction to be confirmed more quickly if needed.

Satoshi (sat)

The smallest unit of Bitcoin, equal to one hundred millionth of a Bitcoin.

Satoshi Nakamoto

The pseudonymous creator of Bitcoin who published the Bitcoin whitepaper in 2008 and participated in early development before withdrawing from public view in 2011.

Sādhana

A disciplined practice undertaken to cultivate insight, attention, or transformation.

Seigniorage

The gain obtained by an issuer of money through its creation and issuance.

Self-Custody

The practice of holding Bitcoin in a way that gives the individual full control over their private keys, without reliance on third parties.

Sound Money

Money that reliably preserves value over time due to properties such as scarcity, durability, divisibility, portability, fungibility, verifiability, and censorship resistance.

Timechain

A term used to describe Bitcoin's blockchain as a continuous, ordered record of time anchored by proof of work.

Unit Bias

A cognitive tendency to prefer owning whole units rather than fractions.

UTXO

Short for unspent transaction output. A unit of Bitcoin value that has not yet been spent and can be used as an input in a new transaction.

This book belongs to

_____

Notes

www.ingramcontent.com/pod-product-compliance
Ingram Content Group UK Ltd.
Pitfield, Milton Keynes, MK11 3LW, UK
UKHW041903230426
12049UKWH00002B/23